JUMPSTART
your
BUSINESS

SOUND WISDOM BOOKS BY
SHAWN DOYLE AND RACHAEL DOYLE

Jumpstart Your Motivation

Jumpstart Your Leadership

Jumpstart Your Creativity

Jumpstart Your Customer Service

The Sun Still Rises

Mo

The Leadership Manifesto (Kindle Edition)

Two Months to Motivation (Kindle Edition)

JUMPSTART *your* BUSINESS

—10 JOLTS—
TO IGNITE YOUR
ENTREPRENEURIAL SPIRIT

SHAWN DOYLE CSP
AND
RACHAEL DOYLE

For more information on foreign distribution, call 717-530-2122.

Reach us on the Internet: www.soundwisdom.com.

Sound Wisdom

P.O. Box 310

Shippensburg, PA 17257-0310

ISBN 13 TP: 978-0-7684-0781-5

ISBN 13 Ebook: 978-0-7684-0782-2

For Worldwide Distribution, Printed in the U.S.A.

1 2 3 4 5 6 7 8 / 18 17 16 15

DEDICATION

This book is dedicated to the memory of Patrick Michael O'Donnell. While his life on this earth was entirely too short, we are certain that with his zest for life, energetic personality, curious nature, and kind and compassionate heart hc truly would have made a great impact on this world.

CONTENTS

CHAPTER 1

GET YOUR JUMPER CABLES READY

"Our lives are not determined by what happens to us but by how we react to what happens, not by what life brings us but by the attitude we bring to life. A positive attitude causes a chain reaction of positive thoughts, events, and outcomes. It is a catalyst, a spark that creates extraordinary results."
—ANONYMOUS

Hello, and welcome to *Jumpstart Your Business*. My name is Shawn Doyle and sitting next to me is Rachael Doyle. It is very nice to meet you. Both of us have been entrepreneurs or have been working in the world of business for over forty years each, so we have about eighty years combined business experience between the two of us.

In her early twenties, Rachael was the founder (with a partner) of a successful photographic studio in Michigan. She also grew up in a family with multiple generations of entrepreneurs who ran many different types of businesses. Rachael used to sit and talk to her grandfather about business and business concepts often. She grew up dreaming of owning her own business. While most girls were playing house and playing with dolls, Rachael was pretending she was the CEO who ran her own company. Her family members taught her many valuable lessons about business, and as a young teen allowed her to work in various family businesses, which were all valuable life lessons she carries with her to this day. She was born an entrepreneur.

Shawn grew up dreaming of starting businesses. As a young teen, he had many business ideas. One such business was a pet-sitting company he began, where he distributed flyers throughout his neighborhood. Even though it didn't work, he learned some valuable lessons as a result. Shawn is a professional speaker, a serial entrepreneur and book author, and he is also the founder of a training and development company that has now been in business for almost thirteen years. For years he has worked for many companies, both large and small, and he has always been fascinated by what they did well and what they did not do well.

All of that to say that both of us have started companies and owned companies, and both of us have worked for many different companies throughout our lives. We get what the business world is all about. As an aside, if you're curious about us having the same last name, we also happen to be husband and wife.

WHY YOU PICKED UP THIS BOOK

There are probably several reasons why you may have picked up this book. First, maybe like us, *you have always dreamed of starting your own business.* Like so many people we meet, you have an idea for a business and have always dreamed of starting your own business. All you need is that one little kick in your cerebellum in order to get you going. You need a push, you need a spark, or even a jolt, in order to ignite your entrepreneurial spirit.

Second, *maybe you already have a business and you just want to make it better.* If you already have a business, congratulations, because that is great. You are a special person in our opinion. Perhaps you picked up this book because you really feel as if your business has gotten stale or you have gotten stagnant in the product or service you are offering to your potential customers. Maybe you have that gnawing feeling in your gut that tells you that you need to grow further or do some things differently in order to have your business go to the next level. You know you are not reaching your full potential—you can do much more than you currently are.

Perhaps you already have a business and it is growing like crazy. If that is you, then congratulations. You picked up this book because you want to make sure that it continues growing like crazy. You also know it requires a lot of work and effort, and you want to make sure you maintain your energy and motivation while you ride on top of this crazy rocket.

Maybe you feel like you are entering another season of your life, or you have another idea that has been brewing in your mind for years, and *you want to start another business.* Maybe you picked up this book for additional ideas. You want to know how to get and stay motivated while running one business and starting another.

If *you are a student,* and you are thinking about starting a business as soon as you graduate from school or not long after, then maybe that has caused you to pick up this book. This is a huge trend now—young college students are not getting jobs but creating their own by starting their own companies. You are wondering what this starting-your-own-business thing is all about and how to go about doing it. Or maybe *you already work for a business,* you have thought about the possibility of starting a business down the road, and you are not really sure about pursuing it or how to go about pursuing it. You're hoping this book will give you some ideas as to whether or not you should start your own business, and what the mindset is in order to take the plunge.

You may have picked up this book if you work for a business but want to start a side business. If you're starting off small, and taking one baby step at a time, then that is fine too. You are hoping this book will help you and your baby steps as you work from a part-time business into a full-time one that is profitable and rewarding.

There are some who have picked up this book because *your Uncle Fred passed away and left you a ton of money*, and now you're wondering what to do with all that money. So you got a hold of this book, hoping that you could get some ideas and inspiration to start a business using some of Fred's funds.

Or *perhaps you are just hungry.* By this we mean that you're not willing to settle for working for someone else. You want more. You have an inner drive and ambition, and you want to create a revolution, you want to change the world—your world and your family's world. You just got a little off track and need a small boost to move forward.

If any of these are your motivations for reading this book, then that is great. We are sure there are some other motivations as to why people would pick up this book too: maybe just curiosity or wanting to learn more in an area they don't know much about. Whatever your motivation for picking up this book, however, let us take a moment to tell you why we wrote it.

WHY WE WROTE THIS BOOK

Why did we decide to write *Jumpstart Your Business*? Why did we attach our jumper cables to this very subject? That, dear reader, is a good question and one that we would like to answer in great detail. There are many compelling reasons why we wrote this book. Here are just a few of them.

It is a big need. Both of us feel as if there are many great books out there on how to run a business, books that tell you how to market, how to sell, how to manage, and how to organize your business. What we have realized when looking at much of the business literature is that there are a lot of great how-to books on the market, and we're fans of many of them, but there was one glaring omission in all of them—there seemed to be no books that we could find that were about how to *stay motivated* while starting your own business.

To use an analogy, a lot of the books about business give you the wood for the fire, but what they don't give you is the spark to start the fire and to keep the fire burning brightly. That is why our subtitle is *Ten Jolts to Ignite Your Entrepreneurial Spirit*. It is like most of the other books look at the body and the head, but they never touch the heart. This book is primarily intended to help you get and stay motivated during the challenging days of starting and running your own business.

We noticed we had it. When we sat down and talked about how both of us stayed motivated when running our respective businesses before we knew each another, we realized that neither one of us needed motivation in starting and running our businesses. The fact is that we already had it. Without sounding arrogant, we seemed to have the innate ability to be motivated and stay motivated while running a business. Why? That is a good question—that is the question we are attempting to answer. What we are attempting to do is to answer that question for you as to how you can get and stay motivated while running a business.

Motivation is a process, not a one-time event. Motivation is not an event but a process that occurs over a period of time. What do we mean by that? Well, what we are saying is that you can go to a seminar or read a great book and be fired up for a week or two, but what happens after that initial flame? How do you stay motivated? What actions do you take?

Our purpose in writing this book is to outline for you the process of getting and staying motivated. If you were interested in buying a racehorse, and someone's horse won the Kentucky Derby, you would want to know the secrets about horse training that led that particular horse to victory. Your business is that young horse and you want to lead your horse to victory. Our goal is to give you the tools, tips, techniques, and the ideas in order for you to be successful. It is our desire to help you keep the drive, the fire in your belly, going strong.

It is a tough world. Look, we know it is a tough world out there. There are many stories of famous people who have started businesses and really struggled for years and years. Henry Ford, for example, started the Detroit Automobile company in 1899. It failed and closed in 1901. Later, in 1901, he formed the Henry Ford Company. Within one year he was forced out of his own company. Then, in 1903, he formed the Ford Motor Company. His third company was obviously successful. But the point is that he never gave up. Likewise, Walt Disney had a string of companies, such as the Laugh-O-Gram Studios and Iwerks—Disney Animation. Both went bankrupt. His most famous successful cartoon character was Oswald the Lucky Rabbit, which was stolen from him contractually by an unscrupulous producer. But he never gave up, and the rest is history. So yeah, it's a tough world out there. You need support and encouragement.

Something we have noticed when starting and running businesses is that there are people in the world who are not necessarily businesspeople (so they don't understand what it means to run a business), or, in general, they are not encouraging to entrepreneurs. Sure, family and friends may be encouraging, but we are fascinated that many people are negative about the idea of starting and running their own business. People say things like, "Well, you know eight out of ten businesses fail in the first five years," or, "I have a friend of mine who started a business and he had to declare bankruptcy," or, "You know, one of our local businesses just closed their doors because they failed." Gee, thanks for the encouragement.

Many people give those kinds of disparaging negative comments to people who are starting and/or running a business. They are the downers. Ironically, these are the same people who talk positively about companies that are wildly successful. They will rave about Zappos or Facebook, or they will take great interest in any of the latest and greatest businesses you read about online and in magazines. They simply admire and praise them. But what about the small businesses that are not the darlings of Wall Street? What about the business that someone is starting in their garage, or working on the weekends to build enough revenue so they can quit their full-time job and commit to it full time? Who gives those folks encouragement and support? While we believe that the fundamentals of business must be followed (such a business plans, etc.), one of the most important aspects of starting and running a business is simply this: motivation. It's the mental part, the heart part, the soul part.

This is new. When Rachael started her photography business in Michigan with her partner, she had never run a business before. (Okay, Rachael did run a lemonade stand that was pretty successful as a child.) But she had drive, ambition, and a positive attitude. When Shawn started his training and development company, he had never run a company before either. When you start anything that is brand new, it can create anxiety and fear. It is a giant leap of faith. Let's face it, when you own your own business, there is no guarantee of a paycheck at the end of the week, which is a different feeling compared to working for a company that is already established, where you know you're going to get a check. It is important to have that motivation to help drive you through the anxiety, fear, and risk.

We admire you. We have always admired and honored people who started their own businesses as amazingly brave people who are the backbone of what makes the world go round. Let's face it, IBM, Hilton Hotels, Facebook, Mary Kay, Kentucky Fried Chicken, Nasty Girl, FUBU, Tyler Perry Productions, and the zillions of other businesses out there did not start themselves. They didn't just one day rise up from the primordial mud, and *bing*, suddenly become a company. It wasn't evolution; rather, it was in many ways a revolution. Some smart, savvy, intelligent, brave soul identified a problem or an opportunity and decided to risk it all by going for it. They worked hard for years and made it happen, regardless of the risks involved. These are the kinds of people we have a great deal of respect for. We get you. Because of that, you are also the people we want to help. The dreamers and schemers and the workers who want to create something new, whether it is a company or a product. We want to help you succeed in your business by helping you get and stay motivated.

Thinking big matters. The way you think on a daily basis as a business owner is critically important to the levels of success that you will experience. It is our desire to help you maintain, adjust, or modify your thinking in order to maximize your success. The people who do well in starting and running businesses are people who have the right mindset, the right attitude, and the right processes for thinking about what they're doing. Dolly Parton, as a young woman, always believed that, no matter what, she would be successful. She dreamed big dreams, many of which people thought were irrational and not realistic. People laughed at her. But her dreams came true. Similarly, a good friend of ours, David Gregory, is an inventor of many ingenious products. At the time of this writing, he has applied for and gotten approval for a provisional patent on one of his inventions. They have not yet gone to market, but if you ask him he will tell you that they will—it's just a matter of time. That is an example of the kind of thinking required in order to be a successful entrepreneur. As Wayne Dyer often says, "You will see it when you believe it."

We have a passion. We have a passion for owning and running businesses, and we have a passion for the concept of motivation as it relates to business. How do you maintain your level of motivation when you have to work seven days a week for years? How do you maintain your level of motivation when what you are doing is not completely and totally working, and it needs to be adjusted? How do you get and stay motivated when your business is failing? These are all questions we have a passion for and want to share tools, tips, and techniques with you about how to address each of those questions.

It is our desire to help you for all of those reasons.

WHAT WE WILL COVER IN THIS BOOK

In this book there are several interesting topics we will cover, all with the intent of hooking jumper cables up to your brain to ignite your entrepreneurial spirit and giving you motivation that lasts a lifetime, not a fire that burns out quickly.

Why Do You Want to Start Your Own Business?

We're going to ask you many questions about why you want to start your own business or why you have a business in the first place. One of the keys of motivation is to have a reason behind what it is that you're doing—why are you doing it? Yes, we understand that most people start businesses to make money, and as capitalists we do not have any issue with making money. After all, that is one of the purposes of the business.

All that being said, we find that most people who start a business start it not only to make money, but there are usually other reasons for starting it too. Typically, their business is something they have a passion for, something they want to use to change the world, to help certain people, or to make a positive impact on other people's lives; others start a business because they want to revolutionize an industry, right a wrong, make something better, make a product, or bring joy to humanity. Throughout this book we will be asking you to think long and hard about why you want to start a business and what the purpose of the business is. It is a powerful and compelling question that deserves to be answered.

Once you have determined the purpose of the business and what the business is, then we will also be delving into what makes you different from other businesses that offer a similar service or sell a comparable product. What is your unique selling proposition, as a business, as a product, and as a person? In other words, what makes you better than your competitors?

Setting goals. Shockingly, research shows that most people in our society do not have clearly articulated goals. Some research even suggests that the percentage of people who have clearly articulated goals is just 3 percent of the population. This means that most people who start a business do not have clearly articulated goals for their business. Because they lack the discipline of goals in their personal life, they also will lack discipline in their business life. One aspect of getting and staying motivated as a businessperson is to know where you are headed—translation, what are your short- and long-term goals, both personally and professionally? You can't hit a target if you don't know what that target is.

Managing your time. The most important asset you have as a person who is building a business is how you spend every minute of your day. Think of your time as a bank account, and your minutes as dollars in that account. Where are you actually budgeting and spending your time, and what time will have the best return on your investment? It is up to you to make your time count to its fullest advantage. As Alan Lakein once said, "Time equals life; therefore, waste your time and waste your life, or master your time and master your life."

Resources. Smart businesspeople and entrepreneurs know where to find the resources they need in order to get and stay motivated.

We will share with you a lot of valuable resources that we constantly find helpful in order to get and stay motivated in the world of business. Some of the resources will be old-fashioned, and some of the resources will be new and hip and cool. But either way, each one can help you in a different way. The key is knowing where to find the resources that will help you get and stay motivated.

Network. The quality of your business and the level of your success will be equal in correlation to the kind of people you associate with. We will take a close look at your associations and how critical it is to associate with the right people for the right reasons at the right times. We will also share the kind of groups that you want to get involved with and be part of in order to maintain your level of motivation and enthusiasm. For example, when Rachael was a photographer she belonged to the PPA, the Professional Photography Association, which was helpful in staying motivated in her business.

Energy. Where is it that an entrepreneur finds the energy to the build a business or maintain a business? Well, it is simple and sold at your local hardware store (okay, just kidding). On a more serious note, the hours of effort and labor and sweat will require a great deal of energy. How do you maintain or even increase your level of energy while doing everything necessary to have a successful business? We will cover all of the areas you need to look at in order to be an energetic entrepreneur, mentally and physically, including exercise, staying fit, and getting plenty of rest.

Revenue. When you start and run a business, nothing is more motivating than money. It is motivating to dream up an idea on a blank piece of paper and watch it eventually grow up and generate money. When that takes place, it is a fantastic feeling. One of the things we want you to think about in terms of getting and staying motivated is looking at your primary and your secondary revenue streams, as well as the idea of creating passive income.

Learning and growing. One of the keys to getting and staying motivated as a businessperson is continually learning and growing. It is not an option to be stagnant. Great entrepreneurs are always learning and growing. In fact, just this morning Shawn was reading *Inc.* magazine. He read an article about an entrepreneur who gave him a new idea about his business. This is just one small example of learning and growing by reading about a new or innovative idea. We will cover all of the different channels you can think about in terms of learning and growing as a businessperson. This also means keeping up with the marketplace and the competition.

Creativity. One of the key elements of being and staying motivated in the world of business is keeping open your channels of creativity. When you are creative, you always look at new ways of doing things, new approaches, and new ways of generating revenue. We will give you some specific thought processes to look at in terms of enhancing and building your creativity to a higher level.

Thinking. The late great Zig Ziglar said once, "If your thinking is stinking you need to get a checkup from the neck up." We love that saying, and Zig also once said that "your attitude determines your altitude." We will review with you some of the elements you need to be thinking about in relation to how you think. As far as we know, we are the only species on the planet who have the ability to think about how we think. We will give you some innovative food for thought in order to adjust your thinking as an entrepreneur. We want you to live, breathe, and think like a great entrepreneur.

HOW TO USE THIS BOOK

Take notes. We strongly recommend that you keep a notebook nearby in order to take notes and write down key concepts and techniques. That way, when you're finished reading this book, you'll have a cheat sheet nearby so you can implement what you've learned into your business. Hopefully, you'll have some notes on how to stay motivated.

Read this book more than once. Research has shown that much more sinks in on the second and third readings than it does on the first reading.

Use the Work It section. Think of this as an area for your action plan. At the end of each chapter you will see a list of compelling questions to work through some of the key elements contained in that particular chapter. Please do not skip over this section, because this is the piece that will allow you to apply the concepts to you and your business.

Embrace it. As you read *Jumpstart Your Business,* have an open mind in order to embrace the key concepts and ideas presented within its pages. If you have an open mind, then you will have a much better chance of getting and staying motivated.

Read it with someone else. Buy several copies of the book, give one to a friend or business partner, and then have a discussion group in order to compare notes. Having a partner can add to your level of motivation. A shared idea is a lot more powerful than one that is solo. Listen and learn, not just by talking but by listening.

Welcome to *Jumpstart Your Business.* Now get ready to jump.

> *"Successful entrepreneurs find the balance between listening to their inner voice and staying persistent in driving for success—because sometimes success is waiting right across from the transitional bump that's disguised as failure."*
> —NAVEEN JAIN

CHAPTER 2

JOLT #1:
HAVE A MISSION AND A PURPOSE

Gotta Be Starting Something

"When you discover your mission, you will feel
its demand. It will fill you with enthusiasm
and a burning desire to get to work on it."
—W. Clement Stone

When Rachael ran her photography business, many people would often ask her, "Why did you start a photography business?" or, "How did you get into this?" It is, of course, a common question for anyone who has started their own business in which they are passionate. When Shawn travels around the country as a professional speaker, people often ask him what he used to do and how he got into professional speaking. All of these questions imply a larger question: why do you do what you do?

Of course, ladies and gents, we would like to ask you the same question: why do you want to start a business? Why not keep working for "the man" in a faceless, nameless cube farm, hmm? Okay, we're joking about that just a little bit, but the question is a very legitimate one: why do you want to start your business? Since this is a book about motivation, we feel like the core of your motivation in your business is understanding and articulating why you want to start a business to begin with. Or if you already have a business, why did you decide to start the business in the first place?

Was it because you want to make money, or you want independence and freedom? Did you start your particular business because it's something you have a passion for, or because you have a very specific skill set already developed? Did you want to save the world and the people who live here, or just save people time and money? Did you want to start a revolution in your industry, or leave a legacy for generations to come? Did you want to build a family business, call your own shots, be your own boss? Did you have a dream, a calling, a mission in life to do what you are doing? Did you love creating something out of nothing or improving something that has already been created? Or was it because you wanted your hobby to be your living, or you wanted a different lifestyle, or change in your life? Or maybe it was because you wanted to make a difference and do work that matters. Even though these are only a few examples, it is important to identify the reasons *why* you want to start and/or run a business. Here is what we want you to do: take out a piece of paper and a pen, and then pretend you have just met a bigwig venture-capital investor on an elevator, and she asked you this question: "Why did you start your business?" Make a list of all the reasons, both personally and professionally, as to why you want to start a business. It is important to take your time here—trust us, we will wait right here until you're done. Write down the little reasons and the big reasons—don't try to edit here, but just write down all of the reasons you can possibly think of.

It is important to have this answered at the outset because this is the foundation of your motivation. It will be the bedrock of your motivation. When you have to work long hours, when you have to travel all over the country, or when you have to work hard all weekend, or early in the morning or late at night, or when you have to sit in some lousy airport in the middle of nowhere, or check into yet another hotel when you would really rather be at home, you will always be able to come back to this answer. Why I am doing this? The answer to this question gives you the motivation to keep doing what you're doing. It is the rocket fuel for your high-performance engine called motivation.

Shockingly, we meet many people who do not have an answer to this question. They just decided on a whim to start a business. When asked why they started it, they have many lame answers like, "It seemed like a good idea at the time," or, "I don't know why," or, "My sister-in-law suggested I should do it." It quickly becomes apparent that they don't know why they started the business. This can be a big stumbling block when it comes to their motivation, for if they don't know why they began, then they won't have a sure foundation when times become challenging.

MISSION CENTRAL

Now that you have a list of reasons why you are starting your business, whether it's a small business, medium-size business, or a large business, the next step is to create a mission and a vision statement for your organization. Before we get into mission and vision statements, however, we need to look at the definition of *mission* and *vision*.

The official definition from *Webster's Dictionary* for *mission* is "a pre-established and often self-imposed objective or purpose." There are a few interesting parts to this definition. One element of the definition is the word *pre-established*. This means that there's been some forethought and thinking that went into the establishment of a mission. Secondly, the word *self-imposed* is interesting because it indicates that the creation of the mission is a proactive activity, not a reactive one. The next part of the definition mentions the word *objective*, and, of course, it's important to determine what your objectives are. You have to have objectives in order to meet objectives. Clearly then a mission and vision statement helps you reach goals by establishing and self-imposing them.

When Rachael had her business, the mission statement was, "To capture each unique individual at a moment in time in their own light and style with skill and grace and respect, to bring forth the true spirit of one's soul." The mission statement can be used to drive motivation with your employees.

The next thing we need to look at is the definition of *vision*. We love the definition of *vision*, which is "the act or power of imagination, the mode of seeing or conceiving, or unusual discernment or foresight." What an interesting and inspiring definition. Did you notice the acknowledgment of the power of imagination and the use of the word *foresight*? It is true that great entrepreneurs should have a powerful imagination and great foresight. After all, didn't Steve Jobs, Martin Luther King Jr., Mary Kay, and Famous Amos possess these?

Having a mission and a vision statement are important, no matter what size company you have. The mission and vision statements are a perfect combination for creating and sustaining motivation for your business. The mission is where we identify any objectives we're going to achieve, and the vision is what we are striving to achieve long term, or where we're headed. Think of mission and vision statements as the perfect combination between short term (mission) and long term (vision).

There are some benefits in developing a mission and a vision statement. The first is that it helps you increase your focus for your business. In the fast-paced world in which we live, it's important to stay focused on the task at hand. Properly executed mission and vision statements allow you and the team to be remarkably focused on future objectives.

Secondly, it helps increase morale. Organizations that have great mission and vision statements seem to have a higher level of employee morale than employees who work for companies that don't have one. Why is that? A mission statement and a vision statement provides ground rules for employees to follow, and it gives a team of people something to rally around. It's analogous to a sports team having a cheerleader or a person going on a trip having a map. When people are excited about future possibilities, then the organizational morale goes up. When they don't know the purpose of the company, then the morale goes down.

Maybe you are a solo entrepreneur starting a business and you don't have any employees. Okay, that may be true, but having mission and vision statements will also improve your morale, and it will come across when you have discussions with people about your business.

Thirdly, having vision and mission statements are important for enhanced decision making. When you have these written down, it's much easier for you to make decisions because all of your decisions will be based on your mission and vision. When you have to make immediate decisions about a customer product or procedure, you'll refer back to your mission and vision statements, asking to yourself, is this what we are trying to do?

Lastly, having vision and mission statements are important to have strategic clarity. They will give you more clarity around developing and executing a strategy with you and your employees. You can constantly ask yourself, is this strategy aligned with my mission and vision? All great organizations have clear mission statements, which helps create the culture and the environment of the company. But all great companies start first as thoughts on paper.

PURPOSE

Once the mission and vision are clear—the short- and long-term views of your business—the next question is, what is your purpose? The dictionary defines *purpose* as "the reason for which something exists or is done, made, or used." That is a pretty solid definition. We already talked about the fact that you want to start a business and the reasons behind starting it. The larger question is, what is the purpose of the business? In other words, what is the reason why your business exists beyond the fact you wanted to start one? What is the purpose of your business beyond making money?

For example, if you were a dentist, you may say the purpose of your dental practice is to bring dentistry to the masses by keeping it affordable. Another dentist, however, may say the purpose of his or her dental practice is to serve the affluent with premium restorative dentistry in order to enhance their image in society. As you can see, these are both extremely different purposes, but none of them is right or wrong; rather, they are just different drives and serving different market segments. This is why it is important to give a great deal of thought as to why you have your business and what purpose your business serves.

UNIQUE SELLING PROPOSITION

When Shawn teaches sales training classes, he talks to salespeople and asks them a simple question: "How are you, your product, or your service different than everyone else?" This is called a USP, or a unique selling proposition. Thinking of your purpose in this way will help you determine how your business is different from others in a similar market.

What Makes Your Company Different?

For example, Shawn once met an owner of a local delivery service at a networking event. He asked the gentleman how his company was different than all of his competition. His answer was "that they delivered quickly." Shawn simply smiled and said, "Yes, but FedEx and UPS are both in the business of delivering quickly—so what makes you different?" He said, "Well, we are local." Shawn then asked if being local made him cheaper or faster, and this man told Shawn that his service was about the same price as the others. The reality is that the owner of this delivery service had not figured out how his business was different from all of his potential competitors. If he were smart, he would say, "I can have any package anywhere in these five counties in less than ninety minutes." That is something that UPS and FedEx just can't do.

We genuinely want you to think about what makes your company different? You may be faster, offer better service, be smarter, more supportive, cheaper, or even more unique. Or you may be more efficient, more productive, more expensive/premium, luxurious, cutting edge, or proprietary. You could be new, old, local, national, or even international. Maybe you're hip and fashionable, weird and quirky, fun, or revolutionary. Whatever the case, you need to be set apart from your competition.

People tell Shawn all of the time that his company makes training products and programs that are entertaining and "not boring," and that he really connects with the learners. People always told Rachael when she had her photography business that her photographs were personalized and unique, which gave her company a competitive edge. Rachael went about doing this by trying to capture the true personality of the people she was photographing. One of the ways she would do this was to get people to feel more comfortable. When they were comfortable, their personalities would emerge and shine through in their portraits. After all, it wasn't just a portrait but a portrait of a unique individual.

For example, Rachael was once approached by a family who wanted a portrait of the entire generation of a family (grandparents, parents, grandkids, and great-grandkids) who owned a large farm. Most photographers would have had them come to their studio, the men would be in suits and ties and the ladies in their best formal attire, but it would have been inauthentic to who they were. Instead, Rachael went to their farm and had each family wear different color shirts with the farm logo and khakis. Each colored shirt represented a different generation. She posed them outside in the sunlit farmland. They loved the photo because it captured their personalities so well. This is what made her photos unique and different. It wasn't about a portrait—it was about capturing the heart and soul of a person.

What Makes Your Products Different?

You have now determined how your company is different. The next question is, what makes your *products* different? Your products could be:

- a new invention (Apple Watch)

- a new process (Vistaprint)

- innovative (Garmin)

- money-saving (Geico)

- time-saving (Stamps.com)

- better quality (Mercedes)

- less expensive (Hotels.com)

- easier to use (Amazon Prime)

- more efficient (QuickBooks)

- tastier (Auntie Anne's Pretzels)

- quirky (Quirky.com), weird (Austin, Texas)

- different (Pandora)

- old-fashioned (Stewart's Soda)

- revolutionary (Airbnb), or market breaking (Uber)

If you open a doughnut shop called Dinosaur Doughnuts, you may have a great purpose behind starting your company because you're going to donate a certain percentage of your profits to help children. But if your product is a doughnut, we want to know how your doughnuts are different than any other doughnut in the world. If you say that your doughnuts are "kind of like" Dunkin' Donuts or Krispy Kreme Doughnuts, then we would tell you that you shouldn't have started a business, because your doughnuts should not be "like" anyone else's. Why should we buy your doughnuts if they just taste like everybody else's? Now if they were diet doughnuts (they had a lot fewer calories), or nutritional doughnuts (full of vitamins and minerals), or crazy doughnuts with flavors we have never tried before (like a shoofly pie doughnut), then your product would get our attention. This is why it is important to figure out how your product is different from others in the marketplace.

You are probably wondering how all of this relates to staying motivated when starting or running a company. One of the keys to staying motivated is the excitement of knowing that you're doing something special, different, and unique, or somehow better than the competition. After all, who would get excited about the same old, same old? No one. Our goal is to help you identify how your company is different, how your products are different, and how you are different. Your business is the only business that has something no other business has—you.

What Makes You Different?

Talent, abilities, and knowledge. What makes *you*, as an individual, different? What makes you different is either your talent, experience, ability, or your knowledge, or a combination of all four of these. Many people are born with specific talents. Rachael, for example, has an eye for design, an innate talent, if you will. This talent allowed her to also be a good photographer because she knew what a good photograph should look like. Shawn had an innate talent his whole life for entertaining people, and he has always felt comfortable on stage. This talent allowed him to be a motivational speaker, trainer, and consultant.

Beyond the raw talent that you possess, which you were born with, comes ability. Rachael had the talent for recognizing what a good photograph looked like, but she had to develop the ability to operate a camera to make it do what she wanted it to do. Shawn had to develop the ability to speak in front of an audience and train them, using stories, analogies, illustrations, and other training and retention techniques.

You may also have unique knowledge. For example, if you have been in an industry for two or three decades, then just the experience of being in that particular industry for such a long time gives you unique knowledge based on your experience in that industry. If you have been a hotel manager for several decades, then you know a lot more about running a hotel than someone who just started working at the front desk last week. They may have the talent and the abilities, but they lack the knowledge and experience.

We bring this up because one key element of starting or running a business is to be real about your talents, abilities, and knowledge. If someone wants to start a gym where people can go and work out, that is great. But do they have the talent and are they good at identifying the right workout routines in order for clients to get more fit, as well as identifying diet and nutrition needs? If that person also has the innate ability to motivate people into wanting to work out more and to achieve their fitness goals, then that is good. How much knowledge of the industry do they have? Have they ever run a gym before? Have they ever worked in a gym before? These are all legitimate questions. If you can identify your talent, skills, and knowledge, then you'll be one step closer toward having a successful business.

It is also important to have the knowledge of how to run a business. For example, Rachael knew how to take photographs, but she had to learn how to get clients, create marketing and business plans, and to run a business that was profitable. You have to learn business skills and you have to learn how to create a business plan.

Passion. Talent, skills, and knowledge are vital to running a successful business, but how do you stay motivated? Passion. You may have a lot of talent, skills, and knowledge; you may have a mission and a vision in mind; and you may clearly understand the purpose of your business; but if you do not have a passion for the business then don't get into that particular business. Run the other direction.

We have seen highly compensated professional athletes who end up retiring early not because they were injured or because they did not have the skills, ability, and knowledge; rather, they simply didn't like playing the game anymore. They knew they did not have a passion for the business. They never did. We actually admire people who get out of the business when they lack passion.

Passion is the driver that will allow you to work late at night, early in the morning, and all weekend long on a big project if the need arises. We are working on this book right now at eleven at night. We are by no means suggesting that anyone should be a workaholic; what we are saying, however, is that if you have *passion* it will drive your success.

Take time over the next couple of pages to answer these important questions about why you want to start a business. We know it would be tempting to skip these steps, but please don't. They are critically important to your business because they will help you have clarity, they will increase your ability to communicate about your business, and they will help you nail down exactly why you do what you do. Barbara DeAngelis once said, "What allows us as human beings to psychologically survive life on earth, with all its pain, trauma and challenges, is a sense of purpose and meaning."

WORK IT!

Why do you want to start a business?

_____

_____

_____

_____

_____

_____

_____

What is your mission statement?

_____

_____

_____

_____

_____

_____

What is your vision statement?

_____

_____

_____

_____

_____

_____

What is the purpose of your business?

_____

_____

_____

_____

_____

What makes your company, your products, and you unique?

_____

_____

_____

_____

_____

CHAPTER 3

JOLT #2:
SETTING GOALS

THE 3 PERCENT CLUB:
ARE YOU A MEMBER?

"You cannot make it as a wandering generality.
You must become a meaningful specific."
—ZIG ZIGLAR

Back in 1962 John F. Kennedy gave a speech to the nation announcing that the United States of America was sending a man to the moon. Neither one of us remember because we were too young, but what we find interesting in reviewing history is that John F. Kennedy did something that was clear: he articulated a national goal that everyone in the nation bought into. This is a great example of setting a goal and doing everything you can to reach that goal. Our president set a goal and got the nation excited about achieving it, and, of course, the goal was reached and was successful.

We believe that one of the best tools and techniques for staying motivated in business is having specific goals set that you're always working toward. Shawn was once working with a group of executives who were meeting in a cabin up in the mountains, a beautiful location by a lake. The purpose of the meeting was for brainstorming ideas for the following year. At this meeting were all of the company's executives—the CEO, the COO, the CFO, and several senior vice presidents.

As Shawn was facilitating the brainstorm with the executives, he asked a simple question: "Let's talk about your goals for next year. What are they?" Silence fell across the room and no one said a word. Shawn then looked at the CEO and said, "You do have them, don't you?" The COO spoke up and quickly said, "Well, we sort of have a vague idea." Shawn then said to the group, "Goals are not vague ideas. Either you have them or you don't. So do you?"

We are truly puzzled at the number of organizations and people across the country who do not have specific articulated goals, whether they are short-term, mid-term, or long-term goals. It's disconcerting to think that organizations are being run without specific goals in mind. How is a decision made if there are no goals to base those decisions on? How do we get employees and people excited and motivated if they don't know the goal we are all working toward?

We also wonder why organizations don't have goals that are clear and that everyone knows. We have several theories about this. It could be because:

- The leaders/founders/visionaries who started the organization did not have the discipline required to take the time to articulate clear goals.

- Leaders of the organization did not think that clear, articulated goals were important.

- Leaders wanted to set goals, but their lack of knowledge or lack of experience did not help them identify what the goals should be. In other words, they were just too new.

- If someone is starting a brand-new business, it may be hard to determine realistic goals.

- They didn't know how—as shocking as it may be, there are people in the world of business who don't know how to set up clearly articulated goals. We have met many of them.

- Avoidance of accountability: If goals are not written down and articulated, they are not accountable to the result.

If you want to stay motivated while starting and running a business, we strongly and passionately suggest that you take the time to write down your goals. These goals will be the gasoline in your tank and will help keep you fueled through all of your days and weeks of hard work. Goals tend to fall into three specific categories:

- Short-term goals: these are goals to be achieved within the next six months.

- Mid-term goals: these are goals that are set twelve to eighteen months out.

- Long-term goals: these are goals that are set three to five years out.

You should take the time to meet with your team (or with yourself and your brain if you don't have any employees) in order to write down your goals in all three of these categories. In each category, you may want to think about your goals for some of the following:

- sales

- revenue

- cash flow

- growth/market share

- product development

- profit

- profit margins

- productivity

- labor costs

- materials costs

It is obvious that different kinds of businesses will have different kinds of metrics. If someone is starting a new website, for example, then metrics can be sales and revenue, but they may also have other categories added, such as unique visitors, subscribers, growth, page views, etc. This means that your metrics are going to be unique to your industry and your business. Please don't be mistaken here: you must have them and they must be written down.

We also believe in order to be as motivating as possible, all goals have to be either:

Measurable, meaning a number can be put on it, or some sort of logical metric; observable, meaning you can see it and others can see it as well; and tangible, which means that we can hold and touch or feel the product in our hands—it has physical reality to it.

All goals have to contain at least one of these, otherwise it is not a goal at all. Let's say, for example, we have a designated goal of improving customer service for this year. So we take out a sheet of paper and a write down "improve customer service." That is a terrible goal because it is not measurable, observable, or tangible. We could make this goal measurable by saying we want to improve customer service in the next twelve months by improving our customer service satisfaction scores by 40 percent. See the difference there? Make sure your goals meet these criteria.

PERSONAL AND PROFESSIONAL GOALS

In order to get and stay motivated, you'll need to have two different lists. One list will be the goals for your company or organization, and the other list will be your goals for your personal life. The goals for your organization should be the goals that you want to see your organization achieve—short-term, mid-term, and long-term goals.

Your personal goals should be goals that, when achieved, will benefit you, your family, and your loved ones. Of course, there is a separation between personal goals and business goals, because some goals may not be related to the business at all. For example, you may have a goal of losing forty-four pounds. This goal would not be directly related to business, so you would not put it on your organizational goal list. But achieving the goal will help you enhance your image and increase your energy to pursue more of your business goals. So both professional and personal goals can work together.

There is one point about personal goals we don't want you to miss. As we stated earlier, according to some research, only 3 percent of the population has clearly articulated personal goals. Shawn often mentions this when he conducts training programs and people react in two different ways. Some people are just shocked and can't believe that the figure is so low; other people argue and say that the figure cannot possibly be correct.

When Shawn outlines where some of these facts and statistics come from, they still do not want to accept the reality that 97 percent of our population does not have clearly articulated goals. This means that most people are flying by the seat of their pants and are doing things without really knowing why they're doing them. People will spend over a year planning a vacation to Disney World that lasts for a week, but yet they will spend no time planning a life that lasts for seventy or eighty years. One of the keys to success is sitting down and having the discipline to write out the goals for your personal life.

If you really want to take this to another level, and you are in a committed relationship with a husband, wife, boyfriend, girlfriend, or partner, write down your goals and have them write down theirs. Then sit down in the living room and read your goals to them and have them read their goals to you. If you can get other people to support you in achieving your goals, then that is a powerful motivating factor in having them become a reality.

If 97 percent of the population do not have goals, and only 3 percent have goals, then having goals that you are striving toward will make you the exception. And being the exception makes you an exceptional person. Do you want to be average, or do you want to be exceptional? When we asked people why they don't write down their goals, they give us some pretty funny answers, some of which are listed below (and they are actual answers we have received):

- "I don't have time to write down my goals." By the way, these are the same people who planned the Disney vacation a year in advance.

- "I'm too busy to write down my goals." This is a similar version to the previous one, but it makes someone sound a little more important.

- "I'm not a goal kind of person; I'm successful and I've never written down my goals." Our return reply to this excuse is, "Gee, imagine how successful you would be if you wrote them down."

- "I'm not into this motivational mumbo-jumbo stuff." Okay, that is your choice. But let's be certain about one thing: it's not "mumbo jumbo."

- "I've always heard it was important, but I've never done it." Let us get this straight: just because you've never done something, does that make it legitimate?

- "I'm not sure that it works." Believe us, there is a lot of data about it working.

- "I've never done it before." Okay, great. We have never skydived or killed a bear with our bare hands before, but at least we have reasons why we haven't done those things.

- "I don't really know how." Sure, but there are 99,849 titles on goal setting listed on Amazon right now.

- "I'm not sure it's really that important." Why not at least check it out? Is your life important?

- "If I don't write my goals down, then I can't fail." This answer is fascinating because it's a person basically admitting that they don't want to write their goals down because if they do they may fail at reaching those goals. They say if they don't, then they can't fail. Huh? The reality is they're just fooling themselves.

A lot of the comments people make about setting goals tend to sound reasonable on the surface, but upon careful examination they really end up just being lame excuses. No one in their right mind would set off in a large yacht to sail across the Atlantic Ocean without navigational equipment. Yet millions of people in their right mind set off sailing every day in their life in no direction at all.

We have talked about the importance of having a list of both personal and professional goals, and that they should be in writing. However, we believe that achieving goals on one side positively and motivationally affects the other side. For example, if you achieve financial success on the professional side, then it's going to affect your personal life. As much as we would like to say that the lists are separated, the reality is that one supports the other. They almost work in a strange symbiotic relationship with one another.

SHARE

If you have an organization with more than a few employees, then you should work with a multifunctional team to develop goals for the organization. Again, these should be short-, mid-, and long-term goals. If you have a smaller team, then this may not be necessary. In larger organizations, however, it is critically important that once the goals are set that they are shared with everyone within the organization. Everyone needs to know where the company is headed and what the goals are.

Both of us are shocked at how many organizations around the world have employees who, when asked, do not know the organization's goals. To be clear, it's not their fault that no one has told them what the company's goals are, and the reason they may not have been told is because their organization doesn't know what the goals are. Share the goals; please, do not keep them a secret. People can't hit a goal if they don't know what that goal is. It's like getting in your car and turning on your GPS, waiting for it to tell you where to go, but not putting in an address.

IN WRITING

This is a question that we get often: "I have goals, but why do my goals need to be in writing?" There are several compelling reasons why your goals should be in writing. Here are just a few of them.

You can see it. Probably the most obvious answer to why your goals should be in writing is that you can actually see them, refer back to them, and use them. Think about how you use a calendar for a moment. You may have a paper calendar (analog), or you may have an electronic calendar (digital), but virtually everyone we know has a calendar to track where they are on any given day and hour, and where they're going the rest of the week and month. No one questions a calendar being in writing, because it works; yet many people question the idea of goals being in writing. But believe us when we tell you that it actually works.

Here are a few guidelines about written goals: 1) they have to be in writing, otherwise they wouldn't be written goals, they would be verbal ones 2) they have to be where you can see them and can often refer to them, and 3) you should schedule a time every few weeks to look at your goals to monitor where you are at in achieving them.

You can review them frequently. When goals are written down, you can look at them on a regular basis. Repetition and exposure to the same information increases the level of retention. Sometimes we hear people tell us that they wrote down some goals in January, then picked them up and read them in February, and they were surprised at how many they had forgotten just in the last month. Repetition continually keeps them in the forefront of our mind, thus causing us to aim for them regularly.

Accountability. There is something real and tangible about putting a pen to paper or a cursor across an electronic screen and printing it out on a piece of paper. It's almost as if we have carved those goals in stone, and it makes them much more tangible and real, causing us to feel more accountable in achieving them. We often notice when we visit manufacturing facilities that there are large signs about safety: 157 days since our last reported accident. It is the kind of sign where the number is changed electronically each day. But if you think carefully about it, the sign on the wall is a goal that has been discussed by management, everyone knows what it is, and it was posted as a visual reminder to hold people accountable to that safety goal. Shouldn't you do that for yourself?

Science. Did we just mention science? You thought this was a book about being motivated in business and now we're talking about science. Are you in the wrong book? Nope. Another reason why you want to put your goals in writing is something called a reticular activating system, which is known as a RAS. Think about the meaning of the words. *Reticular* refers to a part of your eye; *activating* means that when you look at your goals that have been written down and displayed, you're activating part of your brain.

Here is the science part. When you write something down and you look at it often, you are using your reticular activating system. Your eye looks at it and that activates part of your brain. Here is the exciting news: your brain then works on the goal at the subconscious level, even when you're not thinking about it. We have always believed our whole lives that having written goals were important. So you can imagine we were excited when we discovered the scientific concept of RAS, because we finally found proof of something we had always had faith in and believed. It is proven scientifically that it actually works.

All the great thinkers throughout history have written their ideas down in order to process them, think about them, and reflect on them. Think about Leonardo da Vinci keeping journals, notes, and drawings, looking at them on a regular basis in order to stimulate his thinking and his creativity. It is important that all your goals be in writing.

A VISION BOARD

You may also want to seriously consider creating a vision board. A vision board is a piece of canvas, cardboard, or poster board that is hung up on the wall so you can see it every day. On that board are glued pictures of what the person wants to achieve, his or her short-, mid-, and long-term goals. There may be pictures of mansions, cars, money for vacation, the beach, fun, marriage, or any item that someone can buy or purchase, any experiences someone wants to have, a trip they may want to take, or a specific goal they want to achieve. It should also include business goals and business successes, such as a certain amount of revenue, of being number one at something, etc.

Think of it this way: when you wrote down your goals, you used letters that made up specific words, which then made up sentences that articulated your goals. A vision board is the same thing, but instead of being a text version of your goals it is a visual version. The vision board, of course, is then displayed where you can see it every single day. Each day you simply take a minute or two and stare at the vision board, and then go on with the rest of your day.

There's a famous story about the actor Jim Carrey who carried out this concept in a different way. He had a goal of being paid $8 million for appearing in a movie as an actor. So he took a check, wrote his name on the face of the check, and then made it out for $8 million. In the memo portion of the check he wrote that it was for appearing in movie. Every few days he would take the physical check out of his wallet and stare at it, his version of a mini vision board. Of course, you probably know the rest. Jim Carrey was paid $8 million for starring in the movie *Ace Ventura: Pet Detective*. Using a vision board clearly works, as visual cues are another way to stimulate your reticular activating system.

Shawn's vision board has a graphic that says "Amazon #1 Best seller." Two of Shawn's books have now been Amazon best sellers, with more to come in the future. Rachael's vision board in the past had a nice picture of a Cape Cod-style house. When she married Shawn, she moved into his house, which is, you guessed it, a Cape Cod-style house.

There may be some people reading this book who might be skeptical about the idea of a vision board. Sometimes when we mention the idea of vision boards to people in conversation, we get what we call "that look." We're sure you all know what look we are referring to—it's the look that people get on their face when they think an idea is just a little too different. That's okay, because we don't believe that you have to embrace every idea in this book. As a person who is starting or running a business, however, you should at least do one thing—give it a try. It doesn't really cost you anything, except a little time and labor. If it doesn't work, then you really haven't lost much at all. But if it does work, however, then you have gained greatly.

We are of the belief that we have only just begun to tap into how sophisticated our brains can operate. We also believe that many of the future breakthroughs in success and motivation will come through better understanding of adjusting our thinking and adjusting our techniques for getting and staying motivated.

No matter what time of year you read this book (it doesn't have to be January), we are asking you to carve out some time over the next few weeks to sit down and write out your goals with your blood (okay, we are kidding about the blood part—ink would be fine), and seriously give it deep and careful thought. Take the time to write down your short-term, mid-term, and long-term goals, for both your personal and professional life, print them out, and share them with others.

Then we are going to ask you to create a vision board and hang it proudly on your wall. Claim it! You will then see how truly fired up you will be. As Anthony Robbins once said: "Setting goals is the first step into turning the invisible into the visible."

WORK IT!

What are your short-term goals? Why?

_____

_____

_____

_____

_____

_____

What are your mid-term goals? Why?

_____

_____

_____

_____

_____

_____

What are your long-terms goals? Why?

_____

_____

_____

_____

_____

_____

Where are you going to write them down for keeping track of them?

_____

_____

_____

_____

_____

_____

_____

Do you have a vision board? If not, then when are you going to create one?

_____

_____

_____

_____

_____

_____

_____

CHAPTER 4

JOLT #3:
MANAGING YOUR TIME

TIME KEEPS ON SLIPPING, SLIPPING, SLIPPING...INTO THE FUTURE

"Time management is an oxymoron. Time is beyond our control and the clock keeps ticking regardless of how we lead our lives. Priority management is the answer to maximizing the time we have."
—JOHN C. MAXWELL

In the last chapter we talked about setting your goals—short-term, mid-term, and long-term goals. Setting goals are like pouring the foundation of where you are heading, both professionally and personally. Now we are going to talk about the walls that we need to build on that foundation. The truth is that you can't manage your time until you know what your goals are. If you don't have goals, then you are going to build walls on a shaky foundation. If you have goals, however, then you're ready to build the walls, which are made up of managing and prioritizing your time.

BILLABLE HOURS

Shawn once got a call from someone who was interested in becoming a professional speaker, something that usually happens several times a year. The person asked if Shawn would spend thirty minutes with him on the phone and give him some tips and ideas about how to get into the profession of speaking. Because we both like to give back, we often do give time to people who are sincere and looking for help. The individual Shawn spoke to was very grateful for him spending thirty minutes with him on the phone, giving him some tools, tips, and techniques for building his budding speaking career. What happened next was quite interesting, however.

The same person then e-mailed Shawn several times, asking for additional advice, finally sending him an e-mail asking him to review his speaker marketing materials and provide his opinion and feedback. Shawn thought about this and realized that he couldn't invest the time unless he was being paid for it. He contacted the budding speaker and said, "I appreciate your e-mail. I would be happy to review your marketing materials, but that would be at my regular hourly rate consulting fee." The man was then quite offended that Shawn wanted to charge him for his time.

We know many lawyers and doctors who are asked for free professional advice at parties and on the golf course, and they wisely respond, "Feel free to make an appointment and I would be happy to see you in my office during regular business hours." This is a subtle way of saying, "I don't give away my time." Likewise, it is important to think carefully about an important investment, and that is the investment of your precious time. Time is an asset that once spent cannot be returned. Time that is wasted is gone forever, so use it wisely.

As a businessperson, you'll need to be careful about how you spend each minute of your day. As the old saying goes, time really is money. People realize this is true for lawyers who charge in billable hours, consultants who charge for consulting, and doctors who bill for office visits and rounds at the hospital, but many entrepreneurs never think of their time as total billable hours. We think they should.

BLOCKS OF TIME

There is a logical progression from your goals to your time, and there should be a direct correlation between the two of them. There are four areas that you should carefully look at. The first is quarterly. Looking at your written goals, you should then write down what it is you want to achieve in the next quarter. After noting and comparing what you want to achieve personally and professionally, you should put that into your calendar.

It is helpful to think of this as an upside-down funnel: your long-term goals funnel into your mid-term goals, which then, in turn, funnel into your short-term goals. Your short-term goals should then funnel down into your quarterly goals. Once that is completed, then you should write down the task and activities that need to be completed in order to achieve your quarterly goals. Those should then be put into your calendar for the next three months, spread out over that time period. We call these action plans, which are the tasks and activities you need to do in order to get closer to achieving your goals.

The second area you should look at carefully are monthly goals. Once you have your quarterly goals in place, then you are better able to see what it is that you need to do that month in order to achieve your quarterly goals. Again, it is important to take the time and write those down.

The third area is in your weekly goals. Once you have written down your quarterly and monthly goals, then every Sunday night or Monday morning you should sit down and plan out the professional and personal goals for the week, which are the activities and tasks you need to focus on that week. You should note on each day—Monday through Friday—exactly what the items are that you are going to be doing for that day. This simply gives you a track to run on.

It is helpful to have goals outlined as A, B, or C goals, which is a system of labeling goals outlined by Brian Tracy. The idea is that goals are not all the same. Some are A goals (must-do goals), B goals (still important but not as important), and C goals (it would be nice to do these). You can then mark each goal as an A1, A2, A3, and so forth, thus giving priority to the tasks you need to do in order to achieve your goals.

The fourth area to focus on is daily. At the beginning of each day, you should review what your goals and objectives are for that particular day, reviewing your appointments, tasks, and activities to make sure that everything is aligned.

One quick note here. We know that all four of these categories seem like mere technical details, but keep in mind that this book is about getting and staying motivated as a businessperson. The act of *writing down* the goals and then dividing them into these four categories is tremendously motivating because it helps you stay on track each day, which means you stay on track each week, month, and quarter. It is a great feeling to have a plan for the week, knowing exactly what it is you want to focus on and achieve. Translation: it is motivating.

When we meet the cynics of the world, they often ask what the point is of writing all these goals down—quarterly, monthly, weekly, and daily—when they're just going to change. If you were building a house, you would certainly want a blueprint and you wouldn't let the general contractor just build whatever he wanted. Even during building projects, there are changes that need to be made due to things that happen. Even though there may be things that will change or a life circumstances that will affect your ability to achieve your goals personally and professionally, you still need a blueprint in order to be successful. Besides, when you get distracted and have 15 million things going on all at the same time because your business is highly successful, it will be even more important to go back and refer to the things that need to be done in order to not lose sight of the bigger picture.

A SYSTEM

There are so many time-management systems out there that are either paper based or electronic. It doesn't matter to us which one you use, as long as you use one. It could be Day Runner, Day Planner, Planner Pad, Franklin Covey, Google Calendar, Outlook, or any other of the hundreds of branded time-management systems that exist. But please make sure to find a system and actually use it.

When Shawn teaches time-management courses, he often asks people in the group what time-management system they use, and sometimes the answers border on the comical. People say they use a legal pad, 3M sticky notes, a desk pad, or a white board. Some say they don't use one at all, while others say they use their watch or their phone.

No matter what system you have, just choose one and stick with it. The system will help you organize your goals, objectives, activities, and appointments all in one place. It also helps you keep track of your time so you can start referencing how long things take in terms of your billable hours.

If you don't use a system, then it could seriously cost you money and business by not being organized. Both of us have been involved with conference calls where one or more parties don't show up on the call, and when asked later they simply say, "I forgot about the call." We find that to be both shocking and highly unprofessional, and, frankly, if we were the client we would probably not do business with them.

THE LIST

After you have recorded your weekly and daily activities in your time management system, we think it is also a good idea just to have a one-sheet list in front of you throughout the day. This is a list of all the things you're going to do that day, and you mark them off as you get them done. Again, this can be done either electronically or physically, but we believe physically works better because you can take it with you wherever you go. If the list is on paper, then it doesn't have to be charged and it doesn't run out of power.

Rachael likes to make long lists with a fine-tip pen, and when those tasks are completed she marks them out. Shawn likes to make long lists with a felt Flair pen, and when each task is complete he likes to highlight them in bold colors like green or yellow. There is no right or wrong answer here, for we both have found having a list in front of us and marking it throughout the day gives us a great feeling of accomplishment. This means it is motivating. By the way, this list includes both professional and personal tasks.

Here are just a few tips to help make you more effective when it comes to making a list and achieving your goals.

- *Stick to a routine.* People who are successful with time have a routine they stick to.

- *A1s.* You may have a bunch of goals, but start with the most important ones first.

- *Do one hard thing a day.* In every business there are difficult things to do. Make it a goal to do one of those difficult tasks each day. It builds up your strength and willpower over the long haul.

- *Review your goals often.* You should review them on a consistent basis.

WHAT IS IMPORTANT?

As entrepreneurs it is critical to constantly be reviewing what is important. Clearly, what is important this week may not be as important next week. If you meet with a potential large client on Friday and they need a proposal by Wednesday, then the items that were originally on your to-do list for the week certainly would change in order of their priority. As you evaluate your weekly and daily to-do list, you need to look at that list and determine what's important. How do we determine what's the most important?

- *Urgency.* How quickly does this item need to be done? And is there a deadline that is a deadline for a logical reason?

- *Revenue potential.* How important is this task as it relates to generating revenue?

- *Is someone waiting for it?* Is a customer, client, partner, or vendor waiting for your part in order for them to do their part? Will it have negative results if they don't get what they need in a timely fashion?

- *Doesn't align with my goals.* Does this activity align with my short-term, mid-term, and long-term goals for my business and for my personal life?

- *Is it going to cost me money?* For example, filing taxes and filling out forms complying with government regulations will cost penalties and fees if not done by a certain deadline.

- *What gets me to my goal?* Look at the item and ask, "Is this getting me closer to my goal?"

- *Skip it.* If it doesn't meet your goals, then have the courage to just skip it.

It is easy to get caught up in the day-to-day operation of your business and lose focus on the things that are most important for the success of your business over the long term.

RGA

We have had a client who talked about RGUs in meetings, which stands for revenue-generating units. It was a company that sold different products, so one way of discussing the products was by referring to them as separate RGUs. Another organization that we used to work with often referred to RGAs while having discussions with sales professionals. They use this term to talk with salespeople about their revenue-generating activities.

In your business, what are your maximum revenue-generating activities (MRGAs)? You have to know what they are if you are going to stay motivated in business. What are the activities in your business that generate the most revenue for you? If you can answer that question, then one of the ways of increasing revenue is to increase your revenue-generating activities.

We have known people who would drive fifteen miles across town to buy gasoline because it's two cents less per gallon. As an entrepreneur you may be spending a lot of time on something that only delivers a small incremental impact in terms of revenue. Ask yourself, "What are the activities that I need to be participating in more that generate the most revenue for my business, and what are the things I need to do less that generate the least revenue?

When you spend more time on RGAs, then you will get better results and you will feel better about the progress that your business is making. You should be able to tell us two or three activities that are the most important RGAs for your business. We are pretty sure you'd be able to admit that you spent too much time on non-RGA activities and should spend more time on things that matter.

CONTROLLING INTERRUPTIONS

It seems as if we live in a society that is one constant and endless interruption. Between phone calls and people coming into our offices, and e-mails and text messages, it seems as if it's almost impossible to do work without interruption. It is not only important but it is essential to your success to control interruptions as much as possible. Of course, there are going to be times when an important phone call comes in and you will have to interrupt whatever it is that you're doing in order to take it. But it is important to control interruptions as best as you can because they certainly can cut into your productivity and getting work done.

We see too many people who are Pavlov's dog—if the phone rings, they must answer it at that time. That is absolute mythology—you don't have to answer the phone. In fact, in some ways, not answering the phone every time it rings enhances your credibility because it looks like you are a busy person who has a lot going on and that you are focused on the task at hand. This is a positive perception. Here are some tips on controlling interruptions.

Block out time. If you have your daily to-do list, then make sure to create times you can block out completely for uninterrupted work. These are best if they are done in one- to three-hour increments. Turn off ringers on cell phones, do not allow the minutia of life to interfere with what it is you're working on at that particular moment. We are not saying that you should do this every single day, but that you should have times where there are no interruptions so you can focus on your work. This may mean working early in the morning or late into the evening—working the off hours when you are less likely to get interrupted. Not many people call at five in the morning.

Negotiate with your family and friends. We find it humorous that people often assume that because you own your own business you have the freedom to use your time in whatever way you see fit. Don't get us wrong, this is a great freedom you have in owning your own business. However, that does not mean you can take any call at any time from friends and family members. It also does not mean that you have the luxury of having a four-hour lunch, because you have work to do.

It is as if friends and family assume you have nothing better to do. If you work out of your home and you have family members who are also at home during that time, then you must negotiate and explain to them that when you are working you cannot be interrupted. Far too often people assume because you are working from home they can just walk into your workspace and interrupt you. We are not saying that they cannot come in every now and then to say hello or to ask you what you would like for lunch, but we strongly suggest you control the interruptions.

Have a dedicated workspace. Both of us have owned and run businesses that were home based. The one thing we found to be most beneficial was to have specific dedicated workspaces. Here is an important point—when we get up in the morning we change into our daytime clothes, and walk down the hallway through a doorway that leads to our office space. Having this dedicated workspace controls interruptions and puts us in a mindset that lets us know that we are no longer at home but at work. Rachael gets up and gets dressed, does her hair and makeup, and yes, even puts on her shoes. Yes, she could wear her PJs and bunny slippers all day long, but that is not the right mindset to be in for work.

Be careful with television and the Internet. Because you are working from home and other people are not controlling your schedule the same way they would be if you were working in a corporate office, you may be tempted at times to turn on the television while you're eating lunch just to check out your favorite show. This is definitely a danger area because you can get pulled in and end up watching hours of television while getting absolutely nothing done. The same goes for mindless Internet surfing too. Even taking a small break just to check something online can end up wasting hours on the web mindless surfing. Don't interrupt yourself by introducing these distractors into your daily work habits.

Set a timer. Rachael makes strategic use of an actual timer she sets so she can focus for a prespecified amount of time. This allows her to focus solely on the task at hand, and when the timer goes off it gives her a great awareness of how much time is going by and how much time remains in the workday. It also reminds her to work faster, stay on task, and not get interrupted.

Interruptions are dangerous because you don't realize how much they cost you in the long run. If you are constantly interrupted, it may lead you to do one less proposal, make one less phone call, send one less e-mail, which doesn't really seem like that much. However, if you have a bad month in terms of revenue, it's not that you had a bad month but that you had a bad month about three months ago. Each bit of time that gets carved away does end up eventually costing you revenue and sales—you just don't know it while it's happening.

PLANNING YOUR DAY

At the beginning of each day, you should be equipped with three very specific tools. You need to have your to-do list for the day, your calendar with your goals and objectives on it, and your appointments for both meetings and phone calls you need to make. All three of these will help you stay on track throughout the day and should constantly be referred to as you work your plan and plan your work.

It is also important for the people in your life—your family. A great part about being an entrepreneur is that you can carve time out of your day to go to your kid's soccer game or have a date/day trip with your spouse. An advantage of being an entrepreneur is having that freedom to experience things you normally wouldn't be able to if you worked at physical office. Here are some additional tips in order to assist you with your daily planning.

Combine your professional and personal tasks. As an entrepreneur, we do not believe that you can live your life in isolation. It is helpful to have both your personal and professional task lists combined. Let's say, for example, that you are going to make a business-related bank deposit and you take your list with you as you run your errand. While you are out you may also want to swing by the dry cleaners, which is in the same complex as the bank. Now you have made yourself more time efficient because you have done two tasks on one trip, one was personal and the other was business related.

Combine like activities. As mentioned in the earlier example, if you're going to run errands, maybe combine a few errands into one trip instead of several errands in different trips. Try to combine activities together. For example, if you are making phone calls, try to make all of your phone calls in one block of time, then send all of your e-mails in a single block of time, and do project work in one block of time. When you make one phone call, then switch to e-mail, then work on a project for a few moments, it is hard to stay focused on any one task. Once you get into the groove of making phone calls, it's easier to continue making phone calls; once you get into the rhythm of sending e-mails, it is easier to send them all instead of jumping from task to task.

Micro calendar. You may even want to think about incorporating a micro calendar into your daily planning. What we refer to as setting up a micro calendar is to block like activities into your calendar and organizing them in fifteen minutes to one hour blocks. See an example of a micro calendar below.

THE MICRO CALENDAR				
TIME	BLOCK 1	BLOCK 2	BLOCK 3	BLOCK 4
8:00–9:00				
9:00–10:00				
10:00–11:00				
11:00–12:00				
12:00–1:00				
1:00–2:00				
2:00–3:00				
3:00–4:00				
5:00–6:00				
6:00–7:00				

Abbreviation key:
M- Meetings   **P**- Phone   **E**- E-mail   **PR**- Project   **R**- Research

Take breaks. We are often amazed in corporate America that most people do not take breaks in the morning or in the afternoon. At lunch they often take their food back to their desk and work while they eat their lunch. This is not an actual relaxing break; rather, it's eating while you are working. We strongly suggest taking actual breaks in order to get away from the work and return from the break refreshed. Most research shows that people are much more productive when they take actual breaks from their work throughout the day.

Plan for meetings. If you are attending a live meeting and/or a conference call, then make sure to carve out some time to prepare for your meeting before it happens. We find that many people dial into phone meetings and are ill-prepared as to the purpose of the meeting and what it is they need to know. Preparation is key for having effective meetings in order to use your time as effectively as possible.

> *"I have always thought that one man of tolerable abilities may work great changes, and accomplish great affairs among mankind, if he first forms a good plan, and, cutting off all amusements or other employments that would divert his attention, make the execution of that same plan his sole study and business."*
> —BENJAMIN FRANKLIN

WORK IT!

What system do you use to track your time? Is this the best system for you?

_____

_____

_____

_____

_____

_____

What are some of your MRGAs (maximum revenue-generating activities)?

_____

_____

_____

_____

_____

How will you control interruptions?

_____

_____

_____

_____

_____

Do you make a daily to-do list?

_____

_____

_____

_____

_____

_____

_____

_____

CHAPTER 5

JOLT #4:
KNOW YOUR RESOURCES

GOING TO THE SOURCE: THE POWER OF RESOURCES

"The number one benefit of information technology is that it empowers people to do what they want to do. It lets people be creative. It lets people be productive. It lets people learn things they didn't think they could learn before, and so in a sense it is all about potential."
—STEVE BALLMER

We believe that some of the most powerful tools available to you today are the resources at the tip of your fingers by pressing a button on your device (whatever that device may be) in order to get on the Internet. The key to being successful in business is knowing where to look and how to look, and then how to use that information to your advantage. For example, if you wish to be a professional anything (clown, carpenter, or chiropractor), there are many different resources and associations that you can look at in order to provide the information you need to succeed.

When Rachael first became a professional photographer, she joined photography groups and also tapped into other professional photographers as her mentors to help her learn and develop her skills. This is just one example of using the resources that are available to you to increase your success.

DEFINING RESOURCES

Before we discuss resources further, here is how we define resources, which typically fall into four different categories.

Systems. Systems can simply be defined as software or processes that you use in order to shorten your learning curve or the way that you do things in your business. For example, if we want to send out messages to existing customers via e-mail, we could locate several different forms of software that could help us do that with the push of one button (like Mail Chimp, for example).

Learning resources. Learning resources are simply resources that you look at as places where you can learn what you need to learn in order to be successful in your business. For example, if you are a contractor and you join a national contractors association, you may be able to learn on their website, at local meetings, and also find materials available from the association that will help you grow in your business.

People, teachers, and mentors. There are people in the world who are already successful or have been successful in the industry you are currently working in. They are either general subject-matter experts or they are specific subject-matter experts. These people can help you shorten your learning curve and help motivate and inspire you as you build your business. People love to share stories of their successes and failures, and the lessons learned along the way. Tap into these valuable resources.

Sources of information. These are merely sources where you can find information in order to save time, energy, and money while working in your business. For example, if we were looking for a certain supplier or vendor of a product, there are several websites we could go to in order to search for that information.

The key is to locate resources in each of those categories to help you find what it is that you're looking for. Here are some resources that you might want to consider that are generally good places to start your search for information and resources. Keep in mind that resources are constantly changing, so you have to be aware and observe around you where resources are continuing to pop up. They will help you keep up with your industry and profession.

Google search. Google search is a great resource to find out what it is that you're looking for. If we are looking for anything at all, we can simply go to Google and enter a word search, which will often result in millions of results. We can then follow each of these links to see if we can find what it is that we are looking for. While this can be extremely time-consuming, you often will also have tremendous luck in finding something quickly.

The other day Shawn was looking for a video he'd seen as part of a TEDx talk, but he did not save the link or remember the name of the speaker who gave the presentation. A simple search on Google resulted in a link to the TEDx talk coming up in the first position on the page. It's amazing what can be found. At a company, Rachael worked for someone who had a question and needed an answer about a particular product. Rachael said, "Why don't we contact the designer?" She did a quick Internet search, and in less than a minute she found the designer's phone number and address.

Google alerts. This is a service you can sign up for free on your Google account by simply putting in the name of the company or the product that you want to be alerted about. Every time a new story comes up about that company, that person, or that product, you will receive a notice saying that there is a Google alert.

Let's say you have a primary competitor in your industry. Set up a Google alert and every time something happens with your primary competitor, you will receive a notice from Google saying there is an update. This can be a valuable resource because you don't have to think about it every day; rather, Google sends you a notice when there is something newsworthy about that topic. You can also set up a Google alert for your area of expertise so that you will constantly be seeing new articles and updates on your subject matter.

SCORE. You may have heard of this organization before; the name stands for the Service Corps of Retired Executives. The purpose of the organization is to provide how-to resources, templates, and tools to help small businesses succeed. They also provide mentors who are retired executives and who volunteer to help out businesses. This is only one aspect of the organization; the website also offers a host of other tools and resources, most of them free of charge.

SBA—Small Business Association. The small business association is a US-based government agency that helps assist small businesses through support classes, loans, and grants and learning programs. We are sure there are similar agencies in other countries too.

Colleges and universities. There are many great colleges and universities across the world. By their nature, because they are colleges and universities, there are experts who teach there, consult there, or who are on staff. Find out if there are people who have the area of expertise that you are looking for and see if they would be willing to meet with you in order to give you advice, guidance, or counsel.

Offer to be an intern if that is a possibility. You can learn a lot by being an intern.

Online courses. In today's high technology world, there are many online courses you can take in order to learn what you need to learn to grow in your business. For example, Shawn has several courses on Udemy.com, which, at the time of this writing, has over 8,000 courses and 3 million users who sign on to take e-learning programs offered by various experts. Many of the programs are low-cost or free, and they are taught by people who are truly experts in their respective fields. There are several other online learning portals people use in order to learn new skills too. The beauty of the online course world is that you can take the programs at your leisure, whenever you want, 24/7.

Subject-matter experts. Every industry has a large collection of SMEs (subject-matter experts) who have been successful in their field. You may be able to tap into their subject-matter expertise, either through one-on-one mentorship or as part of a group. Find out who the premier subject-matter experts are in your industry and see if you can connect with them.

YouTube. Although this may seem similar to the discussion about online courses, it is not the same at all. Online courses are set up to provide interactivity by watching videos, taking quizzes, and learning in a participatory environment. YouTube, in most cases, is simply just watching videos on a particular topic. However, we are constantly amazed at the depth and breadth of the videos that are available with a quick search. Most importantly, these videos are free and available with the touch of a button.

Try to find out if there are videos on the topics that you're looking to learn more about by searching on YouTube. Once you find a resource that you like on YouTube, it is also possible to subscribe to someone's YouTube channel so that you get regular updates from that particular person or organization. Each time that resource has a new YouTube video available, you'll receive a message saying there's a new one to watch.

LinkedIn. Many people we talk to think that LinkedIn is both a waste of time and also irritating because they're constantly being solicited by people who want to link with them even though they do not know them. It is the opposite, however. LinkedIn is a tremendous resource that can help you find lots of great information and do research. The first aspect to be aware of relating to LinkedIn is the search window. You type in a subject in the LinkedIn search window, hit enter, then it will give you search results of all of your connections on LinkedIn. Additionally, you can do research on LinkedIn about companies too. By typing in a company name and hitting search, it will show you all of the company employees and their contact information. This can be an extremely valuable tool. You can look up information about companies before you actually meet with them, or you can search for potential clients and prospects by using the LinkedIn search.

TED talks. Every year there are multiple TED conferences held around the world. At these conferences various expert speakers get up on stage and deliver talks on various topics that last between seventeen and eighteen minutes. They are all well done and feature subject-matter experts in their chosen field. There are also independently produced TED conferences known as TEDx talks, which produce the same kind of results. You can search topics on TED talks as well as TEDx talks in order to find topics you might find of interest. Again, these are free.

Associations. Find out what associations are affiliated with the industry in which your business is involved. Then find out who they are, their website addresses, and if they have local, regional, or national conferences. These can be a tremendous resource for you to learn more about your business and your industry, as well as to network with others. Shawn is a member of the National Speakers Association and his affiliation with NSA has provided him many opportunities to find resources, advice, and mentors within the professional speaker world. He also has been involved with ATD (Association of Talent Development, which is for training professionals), SHRM (the Society of Human Resources Management), as well as many others.

Reading. There are rich resources of books, audiobooks, e-books, articles, blogs, and presentations available online just by doing a simple search. We are often amazed by the people who tell us they would like to learn about something but don't know where to find that information. Yet with a single keystroke they could learn that information fairly quickly, much of it being available for free.

Libraries. We know in today's world it seems as if recommending a library as a resource sounds old-fashioned and out of touch, but that would actually not be the case. First, many libraries have begun to modernize, many now offering downloadable e-books via your book reader as a benefit of membership. Second, there are very talented individuals in libraries known as reference librarians. Reference librarians are experts on where to find information, whether that be in books, articles, magazines, or online. We have made requests many times for information from reference librarians and have been amazed at their ability to find the information we were looking for. This is what they are trained to do. Please do not overlook the old-fashioned library, because it is a free resource available in your community, which is often forgotten about and passed over. But libraries are becoming much more new-fashioned.

Meetup groups. Meetup is an organization that is designed to help people who share a similar interest gather in groups. It may be a group of accountants, a group of people who like flying model planes, or a group of people who are artists. Someone can go on Meetup and create a group, announce its formation, and then they meet on a regular basis. Go to www.meetup.com to find out if there is a business group for your industry that meets in your area.

Experiment with different Meetup groups to see if you can find one that helps you. If you're unable to find one that helps, then start your own. A quick search this morning in a twenty-five-mile radius of our office displayed hundreds of groups that meet on different interest levels. Some groups include the Delaware Technical Meetup, Chester County Entrepreneurs, Delaware Young Professionals, Real Estate Investors Mastermind, Professional Referral Exchange, Business Accelerator Mastermind, and Self-Publishing for Writers. This is just a small sampling of some of the groups that are available in our area. At the time of this writing, Meetup has 8 million people who participate in a hundred countries.

Lead groups. There are many lead groups in the United States that meet on a regular basis. The purpose of a lead group is that people (often salespeople) get together every couple of weeks and exchange leads with one another. BNI is an example of a lead group that has been fairly successful. The idea behind the group is that no one in the group are competitors with one another, each person bringing leads to the meeting to share with other group members.

Chambers of commerce. Your local chamber of commerce can be a resource in several ways. First, the chamber of commerce can often be a valuable resource for finding out information and contacts that you are looking for in your area. Second, chambers of commerce often offer business development training programs that are reasonable in terms of cost, and they also give you an opportunity to meet other people in the local business community. Third, chambers of commerce often sponsor business networking events, which allow you to meet other businesspeople in the area.

Magazines. One source we find for great motivation, inspiration, and information is business magazines. Reading magazines about companies and what they are doing, innovation in the world and struggles that companies have had, is both motivational and educational. There is another benefit as well: when you are talking with clients, partners, and employees, you will be able to talk about the current business issues of today. Getting new ideas like this helps you keep from getting stagnant. We also like to read magazines that may not be traditionally called business magazines but can be a big help for our life as entrepreneurs. Most magazines now also have a matching websites that can also be a great resource.

Keep in mind that this book is about staying motivated while running or starting a business, and resources can be extremely valuable in keeping you fired up and excited as a businessperson, but only if you take the time to tap to into them.

> *"We are drowning in information, while starving for wisdom. The world henceforth will be run by synthesizers, people able to put together the right information at the right time, think critically about it, and make important choices wisely."*
> —E. O. WILSON

WORK IT!

Based on what you just read, what systems can you use in your business to make things easier?

_____

_____

_____

_____

_____

_____

What learning resources are you going to tap into?

_____

_____

_____

_____

_____

_____

Which people/teachers/mentors are you going to look at approaching?

_____

_____

_____

_____

_____

_____

What sources are you going to use to get more information?

_____

_____

_____

_____

_____

CHAPTER 6

JOLT #5:
BE A GREAT NETWORKER

You Catch Fish in a Net, and You Build Your Business by Networking

"Sometimes, idealistic people are put off by the whole business of networking as something tainted by flattery and the pursuit of selfish advantage. But virtue in obscurity is rewarded only in Heaven. To succeed in this world you have to be known to people."
—Sonia Sotomayor

As you start or build your business, it is important to network with others in business. Networking will motivate you, it will inspire you, and it will keep you furnished with an endless stream of ideas and encouragement from people you network with. Have you ever had a great conversation with someone that left you fired up, motivated, and stimulated by the other person's ideas and concepts? That's what networking is all about. Your business is only as good as the people you associate with. So cowboys and cowgirls, if you have a great business network with other great businesspeople, this will be a help to you in terms of helping you get and stay motivated.

Networking will actually help you in three specific ways: first, it will help you remain stimulated and motivated through the trials and tribulations of owning and starting a business; second, you will also build connections to people who can become future customers, vendors, suppliers, and yes, maybe even partners; and third, it will help give you ideas. This is simply invaluable.

THE RIGHT PEOPLE

One of the key elements of networking is to make sure you network with the right people. One of the ways to ensure that you are networking with the right people is to develop criteria in advance as to the kind of people you're looking to network with. Some of the criteria may include some of the following.

The right mindset. It is important to network with people who have the right mindset. What you have to do is find for yourself what you believe the right mindset to be. We believe the right mindset is in someone who is positive instead of negative, optimistic instead of pessimistic, a big thinker instead of a small thinker, and someone who has your best interests at heart. For whatever reason, you may want to help them and they want to help you. Think of it as someone who is a member of the mutual admiration society.

Successful. Not that everyone we network with has to be a multimillionaire, but it is helpful to find someone who is successful in the industry who can share ideas, tips, tools, and techniques to help you on your journey. They may be successful in both their work and their personal life, or just at work or just in their personal life. It is up to you to define what you mean by someone who is successful.

Creative and innovative. Some of the best people to network with are people whom we call "idea people." These are people who have the ability to come up with ideas and concepts about your business that maybe you had not thought of previously. These could also be people who are enthusiastic and excited about discussing new ideas with you.

Intellectually curious. You may find people whom you network with to be helpful if they have the quality of being intellectually curious. This means they are interested in many things—in exploring, discussing, and examining different ideas and concepts as they relate to different fields of study.

Happy and/or optimistic. We find that networking with other people who are happy and optimistic is an exercise in getting and staying motivated. We both have had experiences where we networked with people who were not happy; in fact, they were the direct opposite of happy—pessimistic. We simply found them to be a drain on our energy and a detriment to our business.

Connected. Ideally, someone you network with knows lots of people in the industry they can introduce you to, or they know a lot of resources that can help you on your journey. Connected networkers are people who are willing and able to introduce you to many different people in order to build your network further.

These are just a few criteria you might want to consider in terms of what you're looking for in someone who would be a member of your network. It's important to think of this criteria in advance so that if you do meet someone in a meeting or at a conference, or socially, you can easily analyze whether or not you would find them to be a valuable part of your network.

Developing a network is kind of like dating—many people who are single date someone because they are first attracted to them, then they later find out they have almost nothing in common. The problem is that it was attraction without compatibility. The same thing applies with networking: you may find someone to be fascinating or interesting, which is fine, but the question is, in terms of becoming a network member, will you be compatible with them and they with you?

A WORD OF CAUTION

It is important to say here to be careful of the person who is a wolf in sheep's clothing. As Shawn wrote about in his book *Jumpstart Your Motivation*, there are some people in the world who are negative and toxic. We describe these people as ESVs, otherwise known as energy-sucking vampires. The goal of these vampires is to drag you down into the abyss, down to the dark side. The word of caution we have is that sometimes these ESVs do not present themselves initially as vampires but as positive people. It is only later that you learn that they are not optimistic but pessimistic. So please be extremely careful in making sure that you do not network and/or associate with these type of people.

Networking with people who tear you down can be extremely frustrating to your personal life and detrimental to your business. An additional word of caution is be careful with people in your family who may be ESVs as well, because they will immediately want to criticize your business and tell you all the reasons why it won't work. Limit your contact with these people.

MENTORS

You may want to consider as part of your networking efforts finding a mentor who can help you along on your journey. When you spot someone who has a high level of expertise and is successful in your particular industry, or just in business in general, you may want to ask them if they would be willing to mentor you.

People often ask us, "Why would someone be willing to be a mentor and give of their time and effort in order to help me?" Well, there actually are good people in the world, so one reason is that many people would be willing to mentor you just because they are good people. Secondly, when you ask someone to mentor you, it often appeals to their ego and makes them feel special. Don't be shy; be bold. If you spot someone who would be the perfect mentor for you, then simply ask them. People like sharing their life's work and success stories with others.

A key in having a successful relationship with your mentor is to define the mentoring process. We generally advise that you clearly define the expectations between you and your mentor before the mentoring process begins. It is our suggestion that you meet no more than once a month, either in person or by phone, and try not to place too many demands on their time, efforts, and energy. After all, they are volunteering to help you.

Here are some good questions you can ask yourself when you are getting ready to work with a mentor:

- Why do I want to work with this particular mentor?

- What do I want to learn from him or her?

- What are my goals and objectives in being mentored?

- How can they help me achieve my goals?

- How often will we meet and where?

- How long will the mentoring process continue for?

- How do I intend to help my mentor, as well as them helping me?

You will find the mentoring process to be a tremendous experience and extremely motivational with the right mentor. It's also a good idea to keep your mentoring process confidential, because if someone volunteers to be your mentor they probably don't want you telling everybody on the planet they agreed to it, because they may be concerned that too many other people may ask for the same privilege.

Some other tips to make sure that the mentoring process works well for you:

- Be extremely grateful and appreciative of their mentoring, which is giving of their time, effort, and energy. After you meet, send a thank-you note thanking them for their time and investing in you and your future.

- Never waste their time by showing up late or not showing up at all.

- Be extremely respectful of their time and their knowledge.

- Try not to argue or debate the advice they give you because it's probably given for a good reason.

- If you agree to meet for one hour, keep it to one hour.

- If you meet them for a meal, then offer to pay for the meal.

- Ask how you can help them and what they need.

- Share success stories and how their mentoring tips are helping you—that is what motivates the mentor to want to keep doing what they are doing.

- Be crystal clear about your goals and objectives.

Shawn was once mentoring a potential author who wanted to get his book published, so he met him for lunch. This individual had a book he wanted to write, and so he wanted to understand all the steps in the publishing process. After Shawn carefully and patiently explained the entire publishing process to him, the person he was mentoring then proceeded to tell him all the reasons why the process Shawn described would not work. It is extremely frustrating when a mentor (who has sixteen published books) explains the publishing process to their protégé, and they want to argue all of the details behind the process.

We don't understand why someone would ask for expert advice and then choose to argue with it and ignore it. It seems to us a complete waste of time and effort. So not only did the protégé argue, but because of the drawn-out argument, lunch also ended up running long. This was unfortunately a quick end to Shawn's mentoring of that particular aspiring author.

REVERSE ROLES

In addition to finding a mentor who can help you because you are his or her protégé, you may also want to volunteer to be a mentor yourself. This is a great way to give back, as well as being motivational and inspirational. You could either do this on a professional level, or you could do this at a charitable or societal level. For example, in the past Rachael volunteered to be a big sister and mentored a young girl. Helping someone else improve their life can be a tremendously inspirational and motivational act. It certainly is something to think about if you can fit it into your already busy schedule.

TRADE SHOWS

Many times when we mention trade shows to people, they often shudder and get an unpleasant look on their face. The main reason most people have a negative reaction to trade shows is that they have not had good experiences with them. But we want you to imagine for a moment that everyone in your industry was all gathered together in one large convention hall, all at the same time. Also imagine that you would not have to drive anywhere to see all these people; you could see them all in one place and all at the same time. Wouldn't that be great? That is what a trade show is. It's a collection of most of the people in a given industry all in one spot. Even if you do not have a booth at a trade show, it may well be worth attending to meet all the people in the industry and to network with them by visiting them in each of their booths.

It is important to be strategic in the way you work at a trade show. For example, get a copy of the exhibition program in advance and strategically mark who it is that you want to visit and why you want to visit their booth. Then ask yourself why you want to meet with each one of them and why they would want to meet with you. Come up with some sound, logical reasons why they would want to network with you and why you would want to network with them. Be prepared to mention those reasons when you meet with them.

Secondly, make sure that you have a follow-up plan after attending the trade show. Collect business cards, then make sure to follow up with each person by e-mail, a handwritten card, or a phone call after the trade show is over. On the back of the business cards jot small notes of the things you talked about so you can refer to your discussion when you contact them. Let's face it, most people will forget meeting you unless you give them a reason to remember you, and those notes can be extremely helpful in making that happen.

FRATERNAL GROUPS AND CHARITIES

When Shawn's father, Jack Doyle, relocated from Florida to the state of Virginia, he immediately joined a couple of fraternal groups. As a realtor, he realized it was important to network. Shawn's father has gotten a great deal of business as a realtor just by being a solid member of the Moose Lodge. In your case, try to figure out what fraternal groups might make sense for you to join, because people like doing business with people they know.

Find an interest, whether it is fraternal, social, charitable, or religious, and join a group in order to network with people in those areas of interest. Our one piece of advice you may want to think about is please do not join a fraternal group or charity unless you actually believe in their mission and vision. You should only join those groups because you truly believe in what they're doing, then, as a side benefit of belonging to the organization, you will have the ability to network with others.

MASTERMIND GROUP

You may want to consider forming your own mastermind group or joining one that already exists. The idea of a mastermind group was originally mentioned by Napoleon Hill back in the '40s in his book *Think and Grow Rich*. The idea is to gather a group of five to six like-minded people who meet on a regular basis to encourage, coach, counsel, and maybe even push or provoke a member of the group. The sole objective of group members is to help and encourage other group members. This can be a powerful tool to help you get and stay motivated.

Shawn belonged to a mastermind group for few years, and it was really great and motivating for each member of the group. His group consisted of five people (three women and two men): two speakers, one consultant, and two people who worked in corporate America. This was a nice mix because each person had a different perspective to bring to the group. They would meet once a month for dinner at a local restaurant in a private room, and each month one member of the group would be the focus of the meeting. That person would bring a handout and documents of what they were working on and the problems, issues, or challenges they were trying to solve. Imagine having four to five experts giving you their undivided attention and advice, all for the cost of a reasonable dinner. Keep in mind that with technology you can also do this virtually and have a mastermind group with members from virtually anywhere in the world.

Rachael was a member of a photography club, and they would get together on a monthly basis and have dinner at someone's home. The idea was to talk about photography, exchange ideas about the business, and to build a network of photographers that could be a resource. What happens as a photographer when someone asks you to do a photo shoot and you are already booked on that particular date? You can then recommend someone you know from your club. But keep in mind it was also beneficial because it would work in the other direction too, as people would often refer business to her.

All of that to say, try to figure out how to get involved in some sort of mastermind group to help you get and stay motivated.

LINKEDIN

Yes, we know. When we mention LinkedIn, the response is, "You mean the website where I keep getting invited to link to people I don't know?" Yes, that would be the one we are talking about. But here is the part many people miss: it is the ultimate network if you know how to use it properly. Think of it as the Facebook for business; it has more credibility than Facebook and is respected in the world of business. There are some great aspects of LinkedIn you may not know about but that are still important and useful.

Search. You can use LinkedIn to search for any person, product, company, or service, as long as they are on LinkedIn. Shawn uses a great SEO person, and where did he find him? He was part of Shawn's network on LinkedIn. His website designer also came from LinkedIn. As a side note, the SEO company is in California, which is on the West Coast, and Shawn is on the East Coast and the web designer is overseas on the other side of the world. LinkedIn made these connections possible. Not only can you find other people on there, but people can also find you.

Information. If you are meeting with a prospective client, you can find a lot of information about them and their company by looking at their company profile before meeting with them.

Tracking. If you are connected to someone and they update their profile when they leave their company and get a new job, you get a notification of the change. This way you don't lose track of people as much. Let's say your web designer leaves his or her present company, then moves out to do business on their own. By following them on LinkedIn, you're able to follow that particular person, being able to stay in touch with them and not just the company they worked for when you had your website designed.

Prospecting. Yes, you can use search on LinkedIn to locate potential customers just by putting search terms in the window and pressing enter. For example, let's say you sell products and services to plumbers. Simply go to the search box, type in "plumbers" and "Pennsylvania," and you will be amazed at how many results come up. It also shows you how many of those results are already in your network (LinkedIn calls this first-level connections) or are already connected to someone in your network. It's kind of like playing the six degrees of Kevin Bacon game. The goal is to connect to Kevin Bacon in six people or less. There are, at the writing of this book, 300 million people on LinkedIn in 200 countries.

Groups. Another interesting feature of LinkedIn is groups. There are literally millions of groups on LinkedIn you can join. Imagine joining a group of people who do the same thing you do, or a group of people who are your customer base. Let's say you sell products or services to people in human resources, then you can join HR groups on LinkedIn and take part in discussions and sharing of ideas. You can ask questions by starting a discussion or answer questions other people post.

By now we are sure you realize LinkedIn can be a great networking tool. In order to maximize your results, however, here are a few things we believe you should do.

Maximize your profile. LinkedIn tells you if your profile is complete or not. Make sure your profile is at 100 percent completion. Not having a complete profile is like being on a jobsite and not having a complete résumé. Your profile on LinkedIn is like your résumé—and here is a shocker, it shows up on Google when people search for you. Now you see why it is so important. You can list past jobs, education, certifications, awards, and you can even post videos too. We have found that many potential customers look at your profile before they talk to you in person.

Link to anyone. Shawn has over 16,000 direct connections on LinkedIn. Often people say to us, "Why would you link to someone you don't know?" Our answer is so that you will know them. Obviously, the more people you have in your network, the more value it has. Of course there may be people you don't want to connect with and that is okay too, like direct competitors or people who are in "questionable" (as defined by you) lines of work. Yes, there have been a few people in certain industries who have asked us to connect and we declined. Keep in mind that others can see who is in your network, so who you are connected to can be "a good thing," as Martha Stewart would say, or not so good.

There is another compelling reason why you should link to people who invite you: to build your list. Your list has value because these are people you can send information to on a regular basis. People ask, "How can it be my list if these people are in LinkedIn?" That is a good question. What you can do is export all of your connections from LinkedIn, then take those e-mail addresses and put them into some sort of contact management program. Now you have a list outside of LinkedIn, which is a great form of permission marketing because the people have already said they want to link to you. You never know where your next opportunity will come from.

Join groups. It is important to join groups that are of interest to you. At this time, LinkedIn lets you join up to fifty groups. You may want to join groups of people who have a common interest, are of the same profession or business, or groups that contain a large population of your potential clients. You should experiment with which groups to join and not join, but keep in mind that some groups are huge, with over 100,000 members, and some groups are small, with only several hundred. However, the size of the group is not necessarily indicative of quality, so you have to experiment to find out what groups work for you.

Start your own LinkedIn group. You may want to consider starting your own LinkedIn group. All you have to do is have a logo, go to LinkedIn, write your group description and all of the details, and then invite people to join your group. The beauty of this is that you can create your own affinity group around the topic that you're particularly interested in. Shawn currently has one group on motivation called Motivation Nation, which has 12,848 members. He also has a group on grief called The Sun Still Rises, which is based on one of his books that is written for people who are healing from grief.

There is a distinct advantage of having your own group: if you have a product, a service, or an offering that you are excited about, then you can send a message out to the entire group because you are the group owner. That message then goes to all of the members of the group, through their e-mail that they specified on LinkedIn, and it is posted online to the group itself. Each of those folks will receive a message that says, "You have an announcement from Motivation Nation." This is the advantage of having your own group on LinkedIn, and it also helps enhance your credibility.

OTHER SOCIAL MEDIA

There are many other social media platforms out there, and some of them are set up for networking (such as Facebook) and some of them are set up for messaging (such as Twitter, Pinterest, and Instagram). Some of these services allow you to send out a text message and some of them allow you to send out a text message, a video, or a picture. Since this is a chapter about networking, we are only going to address Facebook and we are not going to address any of the other messaging social media services.

Facebook. Many people who own businesses wonder if they should have a Facebook page. It is our belief that you should have both—a Facebook page for yourself personally and a Facebook page for your business. This way people can connect to you on a personal level as well as on a professional level. What you want to do is just ask people to like your Facebook page. Why should they? Give them an incentive or a reason, such as receiving coupons or downloading a free report.

The beauty of Facebook is that you learn a lot about people on a personal level and feel like you get to know them better by seeing what's going on in their lives. The downside of Facebook is that you somewhat lose control of the content of your page. The content of your page is not controlled by you, but it is controlled by anyone you have "friended" on Facebook. If you have a relative or a friend who posts their scandalous pictures of their embarrassing Mardi Gras, unfortunately, because you're linked to that person, that content will show up on your Facebook page. Of course, you realize the danger is then that your clients could possibly see those pictures and associate those wild and crazy pictures with you. We find Facebook to be much less professional than LinkedIn, and that's why we wanted to mention this as a caution.

NETWORKING EVENTS

We have noticed that in many communities the local chamber of commerce often sponsors networking events, mixers, and cocktail receptions designed to help various businesspeople meet each other by providing a forum just for that. You may want to experiment with attending various networking events. If you attend a network event, here are a couple of quick tips to make sure that you are successful.

Make it about them. One of the biggest strategic errors people make when they are networking is talking incessantly about themselves. Your goal in networking is to meet other people and learn about them, to see if they might be a potential vendor, supplier, partner, or customer. The biggest mistake you can make when you first meet someone is pitching them on your company's products and services. Your goal should instead be to learn as much as possible about them and have a conversation, not a monologue. Listen for clues to see if they may be a potential future client or a valuable connection.

Try to work the room. Sometimes people who are introverts feel more comfortable talking to just one person for a long time instead of to many people for a short time. You're much better off having a strategy of talking to a bunch of different people, maybe one person every five or six minutes. This way you will meet more people and be more successful in making connections with a larger amount of people. If you find someone to have tremendous potential, of course feel free to spend more time with them.

Business cards. We see many people at networking events who hand out their business cards as if they're handing out candy on Halloween. This is a big mistake. Do not give out your business card unless you feel you made a connection with the other person or they ask you for your card. You could also ask them for their card too.

Also, make sure your business cards are in good shape. They shouldn't be bent or looking beat up, but they should be clean and not have notes written on the back of them. We once met someone at a networking event and as he handed us a business card, he suddenly got a strange look on his face and said, "I just realized I gave you a business card that has notes on the back; I need to take it back from you." This really is not a good way to handle your business cards, and it is unprofessional. It is a good idea when someone gives you a business card to write a few notes on the front or the back of the card about what you discussed so you can follow up with them after the networking event.

Follow-up. If you make a connection with someone at a networking event, within a few days of coming home from the event send them a message via e-mail and highlight a few things that you talked about. If there is some sort of action you want them to take, suggest that in the message. For example, if you would like to have lunch with them, ask them to give you a call so you can arrange to have lunch sometime in the next couple of weeks. It is also a good idea after the networking event to invite them via LinkedIn to become part of your network. They are more likely to do this at that time because they will have just met you.

THE BENEFITS OF NETWORKING

We believe there are several specific benefits of networking.

It is motivating. Meeting new people and exploring new opportunities and possibilities is motivating and exciting. It keeps you from becoming stagnant in your business. You also get new ideas, which always keep you motivated too. When you meet someone who is upbeat and energetic and positive, it's almost impossible not to become a bit more energetic and positive yourself.

You can identify opportunities. You may find some opportunities out there in the marketplace with the person you're networking with. Or you may learn about new opportunities that you are not aware of by talking to that person.

Get business. Both of us have gotten business by talking to people out in the community or on planes, trains, or other modes of transportation. When you talk to people and make yourself friendly with strangers, it is possible to connect and identify opportunities to network. Sometimes, you can even sell a product or a service. Be open to new opportunities and possibilities.

You can find resources. Networking allows you to not only get to know many people and set up a network that has value, but it also allows you to find resources that you are not aware of. Those resources can often be invaluable; they could be a supplier, a virtual assistant, a partner, or someone who offers goods and services.

It makes you smarter. The more people you talk to, the more you learn, the more you know about, the smarter you become.

It's fun. Meeting new and interesting people can be quite a bit of fun as well. Yes, it is true that sometimes when you network you don't connect with someone and that's okay. If you don't connect to someone, there are plenty of other fish in the sea—the world is a big place—this one was not for you.

It's who you know. Often we have found in the world of business that opportunities come about because of someone you know. The first book that Shawn got published was a result of talking to his friend Paul who owned a business in Richmond, Virginia. When Shawn described the book he was writing, Paul said, "I should introduce you to Bob—maybe he would publish your book." An introduction to Bob was made by Paul, and Shawn then connected to Bob and landed a contract for two books, one on motivation and one on training. Those first two books then led to Shawn's increased credibility when he met with the publisher that he currently has now.

When Rachael was a photographer, she met a man at a networking event who ran a local photo-developing lab. She already had a quality lab that processed almost all of her photos (a valuable resource for a busy photographer). She got his business card, and when she was in the area, she stopped in and said hello and they talked about the photography business. As it turns out, they knew many of the same people. She kept in touch, and when she had too much volume and needed a quick turnaround time on a project, she would call him. Because she had established a relationship, he was glad to help her out. Not only that, but she also referred other photographers to him.

These are just a couple of examples of a network connection paying off for both parties. The old saying "it's not *what* you know, but it's *who* you know" is true. It is important to know the right people. In addition, you should also know what you're doing when the opportunity arises. We would think the saying should be "it's what you know *and* who you know."

"For almost the first year of The Muses' life, I would do 5 to 8 networking events a week. And I don't necessarily think that's the right path for everyone, but I realized that as an entrepreneur, one of my strengths was finding the right people who could help us. I didn't come into startups with any network."
—KATHRYN MINSHEW (founder of *The Muse*, a career advice website)

WORK IT!

What will be your criteria for a networking partner?

_____

_____

_____

_____

_____

_____

_____

Who will be possible mentors for you?

_____

_____

_____

_____

_____

_____

What social media are you going to use more for networking? Why?

_____

_____

_____

_____

_____

What are two to three other networking techniques you need to use more?

_____

_____

_____

_____

_____

_____

CHAPTER 7

JOLT #6:
MANAGING YOUR ENERGY

MAY THE FORCE BE WITH YOU: TAPPING INTO AND MAXIMIZING YOUR ENERGY LEVEL

"In times of great stress or adversity, it's always best to keep busy, to plow your anger and your energy into something positive."
—LEE IACOCCA

We are sure you did not expect in a book called *Jumpstart Your Business* that we would have an entire chapter about energy. (We did after all say 10 jolts!) By the way, we are not talking about nuclear or electrical power either. Rather, we are talking about personal energy, which is just as important. There is absolutely no doubt that in order to run a successful business, to start a successful business, or to keep a successful business going strong, a great deal of energy and stamina is required.

Not only that, but people want to be around other people who are upbeat, optimistic, dynamic, and energetic. These qualities are contagious. Let's face it, you just can't be around an energetic person without feeling more energetic yourself. Keep in mind that most people in business do business with people they like, and often the people they like are the people who are upbeat, optimistic, and energetic. The question is, how do we as entrepreneurs build, maintain, and manage our energy level on a daily basis? It is an interesting question, and one that we would like to answer.

We believe there are two key elements to this: 1) it is important to constantly be aware of your energy level, and 2) maintaining your energy level is a daily process, not just a one-time event. We recently watched a documentary about Tina Turner, the famous singer and performer. One of the things that struck us was that everyone they interviewed talked about her amazing energy level—everyone said that just being around her was amazing and exhilarating.

INSPIRATION

Have you ever watched a motivational speaker like Leo Buscalia, Mel Robbins, Les Brown, or Zig Ziglar? Did you notice after you watched them that you felt more energized and motivated to do what you are passionate about? Have you ever watched an inspirational movie like *Rocky* or *Rudy* and realized you were fired up as a result of watching it? Well, one idea behind managing your energy is to identify the tools that motivate and inspire you, then use them to drive your energy level.

You may be inspired by going for a hike in the woods, or you may be inspired by reading *Fast Company* magazine, doing yoga, or listening to classic rock. There are no right or wrong answers as to what gives every person energy, but the key is to identify the activities that spark your energy and enthusiasm. You need to ask yourself the following questions.

What is it socially that gets me fired up and energized? For example, we really enjoy going to the symphony because it is both a social event, a date night, and we get to listen to really incredible music played by amazingly passionate and gifted musicians. The sound is impossible to describe. It is impossible for us to sit there and not have more energy when the symphony is over than before it started. Figure out what it is socially that gets you energized and excited. The other reality is that just getting out of your office, breathing fresh air, or changing up your routine can be energizing as well.

What is it intellectually that gets me fired up and energized? For example, we really like to read the *Wall Street Journal*, not just for the investment advice but for reading articles about new ideas, concepts, and business approaches. This fires up our intellectual curiosity and excitement. Rachael loves reading nonfiction books relating to self-improvement, organization, and personal development. This really stimulates her thinking and leads her to develop creative ideas.

What is it visually that gets me fired up and energized? We both greatly enjoy visiting art museums, lighthouses, and historical landmarks. They are visually striking and, again, get us motivated. We don't know how people can stand in front of an amazing masterpiece and not feel a sense of wonder or amazement or awe. The entire world is full of amazing visuals of buildings and architecture and landscapes and people, as long as you are paying attention and keeping your eyes open.

What is it that spiritually gets me fired up and energized? We are going to leave it up to you to define "spiritually." You may enjoy reading quietly, studying, meditating, doing yoga, or participating in more traditional religious activities. We find a great deal of satisfaction and inspiration by going to church together as a couple. Figure out for yourself what energizes you spiritually.

What is it physically that gets me fired up and energized? This could be running, gardening, hiking, or "mudding" in your stripped-down Jeep Cherokee. Maybe going bowling, horseback riding, doing water polo, golfing, or working out at your local health club is what physically gets you energized.

What is it emotionally that gets me fired up and energized? For example, we both are tremendously energized by being around our families and having good times during big family events, such as birthdays, holidays, and gatherings. Whether it is the love or like of good friends, family, coworkers, colleagues, or partners, find out what emotionally gets you fired up, then do it often.

Looking at all of the categories listed above, make a list of all the things that get you fired up and energized. Then the goal is to work them into your schedule, making them a priority. Because the truth is that you cannot stay motivated in business if your energy levels are low, or if you give all of your time to those things that sap your energy, rather than contribute to it.

Shawn was recently doing a full-day training program with a corporate client on stress management. He asked the people in the room to write down the activities outside of work that were a way for them to restore their energy levels, to relax, and to reduce their stress. When Shawn debriefed answers from the group, one woman said that being outside restored her soul. When Shawn asked how often she participated in outdoor activities, she looked down and said, "Never. I am just too busy." Shawn then said with a kind and empathetic tone: "You're too busy to restore your soul?" She then explained that between work and being a mom and a wife and a family member and a sister, she just never had the time to be outside. Shawn gently suggested that she contract with her family to carve out a couple of hours a week where she can be outside, either hiking or walking, in order to reduce her level of stress. Make sure you make the time for these important renewing activities in your life.

It is hard to do, but we have to schedule activities that help us maintain and build our energy level. During incredibly busy times in our lives, it is easy to suffer from burnout. We find that one of the key causes of burnout is that people are so busy they eliminate the activities that give them energy in favor of doing more work. Let's take a look at some activities you can do in order to build and maintain your energy level.

EXERCISE

We all know that exercise is important, and we know we should spend time doing it at least a few times a week. However, in today's modern world, that is not happening as much as it should be. According to a study done at Penn State and the University of Maryland, on average Americans spend only two hours a week being physically active. This is based on their analysis of the US Census Bureau.

If you want to have energy, you have to expend energy in order to get more—in order to get you have to give. We are always amazed that when we go to the gym, we may not necessarily feel like going at the time (in fact, sometimes on the drive we feel like turning around and going back home), but we know there's going to be a payoff in the end. At a certain point after the workout, we are both abuzz with new levels of energy. We also realize that's only the benefit for that particular day; if we work out on a regular basis, then we can increase our chances of living a long, healthy, and happy life.

The key to increasing your energy level in exercise is twofold: 1) you need to have anaerobic exercise (like lifting weights, yoga, certain types of gymnastics), and you need to have aerobic exercise (walking, running, classes); and 2) you need to find some form of exercise that you find rewarding and/or fun. The main reason people stop exercising and working out is because the exercise they are doing is dull, dry, and boring. If the purpose of the exercise is to energize you, then you certainly do not want to do exercise that is dull, dry, and boring.

One of the ways you can make it more fun is by listening to audiobooks, podcasts, or music while you work out on the treadmill or a stationary bike. This way you combine two sources of motivation and energy.

In addition to giving you extra energy, working out will also boost your self-esteem because you will feel better about yourself. When you are in good shape, you look in the mirror and you like what you see. Then, liking what you see makes you feel better about yourself, which, in turn, increases your level of energy.

LETTING GO OF THE PAST

It is easy to dwell on past failures and past situations that were unpleasant. For example, you may start to work on a project and remember, "Oh, I remember what happened last time I worked on a big project—it didn't work out so well." Dwelling on past failures is most definitely an energy drain. You may have even had past businesses or business partnerships that failed. Fear of failure is draining. Rather than focusing on past failures and negative thoughts, focus instead on moving forward and on positive thoughts. When you are moving forward and thinking positively, you will find that your energy level will go up. It is also a good idea to envision whatever it is you are working on as a success before it actually happens. Seeing it in your mind's eye is exciting and can help you get and stay motivated.

NUTRITION AND DIET

There are so many opinions and ideas in the world about the right foods to eat. We have met people who are big fans of high-protein, low-carb diets, and people who are fans of high-carb, low-protein diets. Some people are fans of low-fat, high fiber, low salt, and the list goes on and on. The question comes down to knowing what the right level of nutrition is in order to drive your energy level.

Well, we can't answer that for you, but what we can say is that you have to find out what works for you. Some people do very well eating more protein and less carbs. Some people do better following a plan similar to Weight Watchers. The biggest question that you have to answer is what level of diet and nutrition will give you the highest level of energy. Having said all that, however, there are a few things that are absolutely true no matter what your preferences are regarding nutrition and diet.

Ideal weight. Maintaining your ideal weight gives you a higher level of energy, because being overweight tends to lead to energy drain. For example, we both went on Weight Watchers and lost considerable amounts of weight (Shawn lost fifty-four pounds and Rachael lost forty pounds, and we are still improving), which increased our level of energy.

Whole foods. Almost every expert on the planet agrees that eating whole foods gives you more energy. Foods that tend to be more natural (such as fruits and vegetables), and foods that have not been processed to death, tend to give you more energy when you eat them.

Junk food. Most everyone can agree that junk food may give you a temporary boost due to the high level of sugar and fat, but it is only a short-term boost and is not actually converted to long-term energy. We know the old adage "garbage in, garbage out." Have you ever noticed that people who eat Twinkies all the time often end up looking like a Twinkie? Both of us have known younger people who thought they could survive on a diet of junk food in their younger days, which seemed to be true, but alas in their later years it has caught up with them in the form of weight gain, low energy, and disease. We are not saying you have to be perfect—just try your best.

Having a plan. Having an eating plan to maintain your level of energy is a good idea as well, so you have to decide what that is. The idea behind having a plan is to help with your energy level and also to be consciously aware of your eating, not just eating without thinking about it. It's not a diet; rather, it's an energy eating plan.

This is something that we want you to think about.

LEARNING

It may seem odd to include learning in a chapter about increasing and/or maintaining your energy level, but we believe that learning new things creates excitement and passion, and excitement and passion increases your level of energy. You need to ask yourself what it is that you want to learn about and that excites you. When thinking about learning to increase your energy levels, here are some things to consider.

What new skills would you like to learn, both personally or professionally? You may decide that you want to learn more about your chosen field by getting more education or training, or you may decide to take up karate and go for your black belt. Either way, learning new skills is going to be extremely stimulating and motivating. For example, Rachael is an avid photographer and at one point made her living in photography. So if Rachael reads a book about photographic techniques, visits a camera store, or takes a new photography technique class, it is extremely exciting for her to learn those new skills.

What new ideas or philosophies would you like to learn more about? You may be interested in many schools of thought or different philosophies. The question is, what is it that you're interested in that you'd like to know more about or in greater depth? And these ideas or philosophies could be related to your work, or they could be related only to your personal interests. For example, for work you may want to learn more about creative and critical thinking, but at home you may want to learn more about great philosophers and how they thought. Again, when you learn about new ideas or philosophies, it stimulates your thinking, which, in turn, increases your level of energy.

What knowledge on what subject would you like to increase? We find ourselves fascinated by many things, and sometimes we discuss the fact that we are "intellectually curious." People who are intellectually curious have an interest in many things and are often asking questions about the things around them. An intellectually curious person going on a hike sees an abandoned old stone house and wonders how it got there, who lived there, and how long it has been there. A person who is not intellectually curious will walk by the stone house and have no real interest in knowing more about it.

What are you intellectually curious about? What would you like to know more about? This seeking of knowledge may be professional knowledge (if you run a repair center and you'd like to know more about the history of certain model of car, then that would be an example of increasing your knowledge on that particular topic), or in your personal life (you may want to increase your level of knowledge about finances so that you can do a better job managing your money at home). How would having this knowledge help you? If you are not intellectually curious, then you may want to ask yourself why. One of the reasons may be that the subjects and activities you're participating in are just not ones that are interesting to you. The key is to find out what you are interested in so you can be intellectually curious.

You have skills, ideas, and knowledge. The next step is to take the time to sit down and plan out what skills you want or need to improve, what ideas you would like to know more about, and what knowledge you need to increase. Then come up with your own learning plan and put it in writing. In chapter 4 we mentioned many resources that are available to you that are free or that are inexpensive, so don't let a lack of resources be your excuse for not learning. Resources are not lacking in today's modern technologically driven world. Give us any topic and we will find thousands of books, YouTube videos, white papers, and presentations—and much more—just by doing a quick search on the Internet. And those are just resources available online.

Don't be intimidated by the time element either. You can do this in small chunks—small twenty minutes pieces at a time. It doesn't have to be all at once in order for it to be effective or in order for it to be called learning. Little bits here and there add up over time, thus increasing your knowledge and your energy level.

LIFE BALANCE

The term *life balance* is a popular term in our society today. To be honest with you, we are not really sure if life balance really exists. In fact, we do not believe that there really is such a thing as life balance. The reality is this, however: there are weeks you're going to work a lot of hours just because your business demands it. Then there are weeks you're going to work fewer hours because your business does not demand it.

There are going to be times when you work seven days a week for months or even years without taking a break, then there are also going to be times when you can take weeks off at a time because you have the freedom of owning your own business. There may be times when a family member is ill or something happens in your family that creates tragedy or adversity—during those times you obviously will not have balance among each area of your life.

Even though we like the idea of having life balance (it is very appealing), it is a philosophy or an idea that is often extremely hard to achieve, perhaps even impossible. We thought you would appreciate this refreshing dose of honesty. Here are a couple of myths about life balance.

Myth #1: Life balance is achieved. Let us be honest with you: life balance is never achieved. You may have the perfect week where everything is balanced, and then suddenly a big client wants a proposal by Friday and you're on the road for five days in a row. Well, there goes life balance. The cynics of the world would say to tell the client that they will have to wait for their proposal, but the reality is that in the world of business you have to seize opportunity as it comes.

Myth #2: Life is always going to be perfect. Life is never going to be perfect because life is full of surprises, and it is full of other creatures called human beings. Because human beings are not perfect, life is never going to be perfect. There is beauty in that. They're going to be flights that are going to be delayed, people who disappoint you, contracts that don't get signed, mistakes that get made, and schedules that get changed by clients without our permission. But it makes life interesting, fun, and challenging. If everything was perfect, then life would actually be pretty boring because there would be little or no challenges. We are imperfect people, which is okay.

Myth #3: Other people have life balance. Yes, there are people in the world who claim that their lives are perfectly balanced, and if that is true, then good for them. We find ourselves skeptical of people who claim their life is perfectly balanced all of the time. Most people's lives are not as good as their Facebook postings claim to be. Most people are not Martha Stewart, and we are not even sure if Martha Stewart is

Martha Stewart, at least how she portrays herself to be on television. We are sure she has a staff of people who help her get things done.

Don't get us wrong here: we are not pessimists but optimists. But we also don't think that people's lives, at least the way they look on the outside, are necessarily the way they look on the inside. Please don't be fooled by the man behind the curtain. When you understand that this is the way life is, then you don't put a bunch of pressure on yourself trying to be perfect like other people. As Beyoncé once said, "If everything was perfect, you would never learn and you would never grow."

Myth #4: Every part of your life is always going to be balanced. There are going to be weeks when you have time to work out four times that week and when you have time to pay attention to your optimal levels of nutrition and sleep. Then there will be other times, due to business and family pressures, that it just will not happen. Shawn recently traveled on a business trip to New York, and, due to various delays and logistics, he did not arrive at his hotel until ten o'clock at night. Unfortunately, he had not eaten dinner and room service in the hotel was closed, and all the restaurants around him in that area were closed too. That night Shawn had to order takeout food from a local restaurant. Shawn did not have the nutritional balance he craved; rather, he decided he would do the best he could. The sooner you get over the myth that life is always going to be balanced, the better off you are. As we often say, "Oh well, it is what it is." Having that kind of acceptance will greatly reduce your level of stress.

Myth #5: There is a definition of life balance. There are many definitions out there in literature of life balance. We really don't believe there is a perfect definition, and we also believe that the definition is different for each person. Don't worry about other people's definitions; rather, decide and define what it means for you, because that is all that really matters. This is your life, right? You are the architect of your own life.

BENEFITS OF HIGH ENERGY LEVELS

Having a high energy level will help you in many ways. First, it will help you be more productive. You will not only be able to work more hours, but you will be able to get more done in the hours that you do work. You will also become more persuasive. People who have a high level of energy are persuasive in the way that they talk, walk, move, and communicate. Most great salespeople have a high level of energy as well.

Another benefit of having high energy levels is that you will feel good. When you have a high level of energy, then you'll feel good about your work and your life. When you don't feel good about your work and your life, guess what? It shows. Do what is necessary to ignite your fire. Next benefit of having high energy levels is that it is motivating. If you have employees who report to you, then, as a leader, your energy level will help them feel more motivated and enthusiastic about the job they have been assigned to do. Your energy level as a leader can end up transferring to your employees.

Another benefit of having a high level of energy is that you will sell more. Most people want to deal with someone who loves what they do, and many times we have bought a product or service from someone because they had such passion, enthusiasm, and energy about the product, which convinced us to buy it. Life also becomes more relevant as a result of high energy levels. Let's face it, life is short and we do not want to sit around, moping, sulking, or moving at a slow pace, having no energy. People who have energy feel as if what they are doing is relevant. Last but not least, another benefit of having high energy is that you will have more fun.

Those are just a few of the benefits of having a high energy level. It is your responsibility to manage and maintain your energy level if you want to be successful in the world of business. Business is not a sprint; it's a marathon. And you have to be prepared to have the stamina to run the race over the long haul.

Because this chapter is about building and maintaining your energy, what we want you to think about is to try to find and strike a balance between work and relaxation. As the old saying goes, "Too much work and not enough play makes Jack a dull boy," we believe that too much work without rest and relaxation is bad for you and causes stress, tension, and burnout.

On the other hand, too much relaxation and too much time off leads to people being bored. How many of us know someone who has retired saying that they're going to "play golf every day" and really are not going to do anything else? They eventually get bored after about two months of playing golf every day because they're not engaged in the real world. This is why it is important to find a balance between working and taking time off.

Think of a seesaw on a children's playground in regards to striking the right balance between work and play. Every time a child sitting on each end pushes with their legs their seat goes up and the other seat goes down. That is how we see the idea of life balance. When the seesaw is sitting on one end too long, then the person is stuck at the top arc of the seesaw and can't get down. The idea is for the seesaw to swing back and forth, back and forth, creating a good balance that goes back and forth.

Here are some questions you may want to ask yourself, not to achieve life balance but to keep the motion going back and forth. Some days we work a lot of hours and some days we don't. Some days we work no hours at all, and some days we work twenty hours.

- How much time do you work per week? Why?

- How much time do you want to work per week? Why?

- How much time do you take off each week? Why?

- How much time do you wish to spend on the following areas of your life each week?
  - Health/Fitness
  - Love
  - Intellectual
  - Spiritual
  - Social
  - Financial
  - Cultural
  - Family
  - Sports
  - Relaxation
  - Civic

If you decide in advance how you want to spend your time in these various categories, then you can at least aim to have more balance and spend more time on the things that you are missing or are important to you. As always, feel free to create your own categories if these don't feel like the right categories for you.

People who are successful and have a high level of energy are not frustrated because they don't feel like they're neglecting a part of their life that is important to them. Keep in mind that all of the decisions about where you want to spend time in your life are completely up to you—there are no right or wrong answers for every single person. If you feel like you are distributing the way you spend your time to the appropriate areas of your life, and you can feel good about it, then you have a high level of energy.

PEOPLE

One other consideration of managing your energy level is people. We have always believed that the quality of your life is greatly affected by the kind of people you associate with on a regular basis. You can and must pick your associations wisely. If you want to have a high level of energy, then surround yourself with positive, motivated, and upbeat people.

As Shawn talks about in his bestseller book *Jumpstart Your Motivation*, there are certain kinds of people we refer to as ESVs—energy-sucking vampires. These people are continually negative, pessimistic, or mean, and we strongly recommend that you limit your contact with these kinds of people. Some people will often say to us, "Well, I can't pick my friends and associates." That is what you've decided to believe but it is not the truth. The truth of the matter is that you decide every day whom you make friends with, whom you keep as friends, and who has driven you crazy for years.

What about your family? Yes, we know you can't pick your family—they are cards you've already been dealt in life. However, almost every family has people who are energy-sucking vampires. They may be a mom or dad, or they may be a brother or a sister, or they may be an uncle or a nephew or a niece or a cousin—but almost every family has at least one or two. If you have a family member who is continually negative and constantly difficult to deal with, limit your contact to Thanksgiving dinner. Go, smile, pass the gravy, and get the heck out. These people sneak up from behind you and suck out all of your positive energy before you realize it.

Our strong advice is that if you have friends who are energy-sucking vampires, then you should eliminate them from your life; if you have family who are energy-sucking vampires, then you should limit the contact you have with them. You do not have to be around them—that is a choice. Being a family member is not a right; it is a privilege. We urge you to seriously consider the impact these folks will have on your life as you try to start and/or build your business. This is the equivalent of jumping into a lake with an anchor tied to your body. You don't need their heavy weight dragging you down; what you need are people who will pull you up and make you feel good about yourself.

Shawn's best friend (and Rachael's good friend) is a guy by the name of David Gregory. Unfortunately, however, Dave and Shawn live in different states. When Shawn calls Dave, he is always positive, always upbeat, and always supportive. At the end of the call with Dave, he feels better about himself than before the call started. That is a definition of a good, supportive, and motivating friend. Rachael's best friend (and Shawn's good friend) Julie O'Donnell is exactly the same way. Rachael describes her by saying that when Julie walks into the room, she lights it up. She always has good things to say, is always looking at the glass as half full instead of half empty. They are both always supportive and encouraging, and each of them greatly contributes to both of our energy levels.

> *"Even though you may want to move forward in your life, you may have one foot on the brakes. In order to be free, we must learn how to let go. Release the hurt. Release the fear. Refuse to entertain your old pain. The energy it takes to hang onto the past is holding you back from a new life. What is it you would let go of today?"*
> —MARY MANIN MORRISSEY

WORK IT!

What are you going to do—socially, visually, spiritually, physically, and emotionally—to get more fired up and energized?

_____

_____

_____

_____

_____

_____

What do you need to let go of in the past?

_____

_____

_____

_____

_____

_____

What new subject do you want to learn?

_____

_____

_____

_____

_____

_____

Where are you in terms of life balance? What do you want to change?

_____

_____

_____

_____

_____

_____

CHAPTER 8

JOLT #7:
MONEY IS MOTIVATING

SHOW ME THE MONEY

"Money equals freedom."
—KEVIN O'LEARY

We sometimes hear the news media and commentators complaining about the fact that certain companies or a particular CEO "made too much money." They act as if making money, or making too much money, as a business is a crime. When did this suddenly become a crime? As proud capitalists, we believe in capitalism, and we believe that the purpose of a business is to make money, help people, and perhaps even change the world. But don't miss this point: if the company does not make money, then they can't do the rest—the money simply isn't there to bring change to the world.

Since this book is about getting and staying motivated while running a business, what in the world does money and revenue have to do with getting and staying motivated? Well, it is simple. When you generate revenue and are paid well, it is a form of *reward*. And when you are rewarded, you feel good and acknowledged for your efforts. It's like going to the gym and starting to notice you're building muscles—all of your hard work is beginning to pay off. Revenue is kind of like building your business muscles.

Likewise, when you *accomplish* your goals in a business, those goals are then rewarded with revenue. It is a great feeling to accomplish what it is you set out to achieve. When you are generating solid revenue and cash flow in your business, it gives you the *freedom* to make many different choices, and that also is a great and motivating feeling. We have always believed that one of the greatest things about having money is that it generates something more important— freedom of choice.

When your business is financially healthy and generating revenue, then you have the ability to *help other people* in the form of hiring employees, giving bonuses, and also helping other people support their families, which is also a great feeling. You can also afford to help charities.

We are sure we can all agree on this simple rule: revenue is good, while not making revenue is bad. When you are not generating revenue, then you don't feel rewarded, you don't feel a sense of accomplishment, and you certainly have less freedom in what it is that you do. Your choices are limited.

PRIMARY REVENUE

If you are starting a business or have an existing business, there are several things that we want you to think about in terms of revenue.

The first is primary revenue. There is the big question of what your *primary* source of revenue is going to be. For example, when Rachael was a professional photographer and had a photography studio, she had several sources of revenue. In the beginning of her photography business, her primary source of revenue was wedding photography. As her business matured, however, she eventually switched from a primary source of dollars generated by wedding photography to dollars generated by commercial and portrait photography. The question you have to ask yourself when you start your business is, what is going to be your primary source of revenue?

Let's say, for example, that you open an ice cream shop called We All Scream for Ice Cream. In your ice cream shop you sell ice cream, and you also have a lunch business, selling soups and sandwiches, and a breakfast business where you sell breakfast sandwiches, bagels, and coffee. Is your primary source of revenue going to be ice cream or the sandwiches? Is it going to be ice cream, or is it going to be bagels and coffee? There is no right or wrong answers here. It is entirely possible that the ice cream shop makes much more money on sandwiches than they do on ice cream.

As an observation, it seems that we see a lot of businesses who really quite haven't defined what they want their primary source of revenue to be. They are trying to do too many things, trying to be too many things to too many people, and the result is that they don't focus on their primary source of revenue. Knowing what your primary source of revenue will be helps you know what to work on, when to work on it, and to know what's important.

Really take the time to sit down and analyze the primary revenue sources of your business. Here are some factors for helping you decide what your primary revenue source will be.

- Good profit margins: your primary source of revenue should certainly have products or services that contain good, healthy profit margins.

- Demand: if your primary source of revenue is going to be a product that is not in high demand in the marketplace, then you're going to have a problem generating enough revenue.

- The market: where are you going to find the customers who will be investing in your primary source of revenue on a frequent and consistent basis?

- Expertise: do you have expertise in the arena of your primary source of revenue? For example, our buddy Steve Shultz, publisher of *Business 2 Business* magazine (a business magazine in our area), has a ton of experience in marketing and publishing.

- Cash flow: will the purchase of these primary sources of revenue generate frequent cash flow for the business?

These are some of the questions you can ask in order to help you evaluate what your primary product or service may be. By the way, there are many businesses that start out thinking that their primary source of revenue will be one item and then they realize a little later on that instead it's going to be a different item, product, or service. For example, Amazon started out only selling books and then later switched to being an online retailer selling almost everything else.

KNOWING WHAT YOU KNOW

Once you have had a chance to think through the primary source of revenue for your business, then it is time to do your research. First, you need to know the industry. If you are starting or running a business you already have a good deal of experience in, then you may already know what the revenue potentials are or what they have been. If that's the case, then you're one step ahead of the game.

Second, as you think about revenue, make sure to do the appropriate research in order to find out if your projections on revenue are accurate. We have found in our experience that most people starting businesses overestimate the potential revenue, particularly in the early days of starting their business. Most entrepreneurs also underestimate the amount of capital needed to run the business initially. So do your research. Where can you research to find out revenue potentials? Here are a few ideas.

SCORE. Try to find out if there is a SCORE office somewhere in your area. As mentioned earlier, SCORE is a service for small businesses where you can get coaching from retired executives and run your ideas by them. By sitting down and reviewing your business plan and revenue with someone with experience, you can learn a great deal.

Mentors. If you can find someone who is already in the business that you want to work in, and who can share their inside secrets with you, then you are one step ahead of the game. Working your network, try to find people in the industry who would be willing to have lunch or coffee with you so you can ask them detailed questions. When Shawn first got into the professional speaking business, he joined the National Speakers Association, then made contact with speakers he had hired when he was in corporate America and asked if they would have coffee with him when he was at the national conference. Many of those folks did and gave Shawn great advice about starting his business as a professional speaker and trainer.

The Internet. Do a great deal of research on the Internet by looking up your topic. It is amazing to find that there are often presentations, white papers, articles, and videos all relating to what it is that you're looking for. Tap into the resources that are available to you, many of which are free.

Research librarian. As mentioned in an earlier chapter, public libraries have a specially trained person who works there called a research librarian. Go to the library, ask for the research librarian, and tell them what it is that you're looking for. You would be amazed by how great they are at finding a plethora of information relating to what it is that you're looking for. Think of research librarians as a human search engine who can find information for you, in physical book form, online, as well as in other periodicals, white papers, and reports. These talented people can be a tremendous asset to you.

Associations. As we have already mentioned, networking associations can be a valuable resource. One of the main reasons why associations can be a valuable resource is because they often have industry-related periodicals that go into great detail about that business in that particular industry. If you become a member these of associations, they also often have white papers, studies, and research you can tap into to learn more about your industry.

Chambers of commerce. In many areas of the country, many chambers of commerce have a lot of great information and resources available to you, including periodicals, studies, research, and perhaps, most importantly, their members have much experience and background. Go to your local chamber of commerce, tell them that you live in the area, tell them what exactly it is that you're looking for, and see how they can help you.

Government agencies. In certain industries, government agencies can be a tremendous resource because of the information they have available for free to taxpayers. For example, if you own a small business, the SBA (Small Business Administration) has several valuable resources available to someone who is starting or running a small business. There are also many resources available, such as grants, and if you are in a certain business category (woman owned, minority owned) you may also qualify for other programs and benefits.

PRICING TIERS

Let's think about American Express for a moment. If you have ever had an American Express card, you realize that American Express comes in many different levels. For example, you can get an American Express card in the green version, gold version, platinum version, and you may not have heard of it, but there is also an American Express black card that is available only to exclusive clients who spend more than $100,000 a month. Just imagine paying that billing statement off every month.

Why does American Express offer pricing tiers? It is because they are trying to use their pricing in order to hit every different level in the marketplace. Recently they've even offered a credit card through Walmart to hit a different economic demographic altogether, who perhaps would not be attracted to the higher fee of regular American Express cards. Consumers are given a choice. Kind of like a fast-food restaurant that offers a small, medium, and large drink, when you give people choices they may select the medium or the large, not always the small. This helps increase your overall sales and revenue.

When Shawn is being hired to speak, the client could just pay for Shawn to come and speak, doing a keynote at the conference, which would be equivalent to American Express' green level. However, the client can also choose to buy one copy of Shawn's book for each person, which would be perceived as the gold level. In addition to having Shawn speak and getting a copy of Shawn's book for each person, they could also purchase one of Shawn's e-learning courses for each person as well. This would be known as the platinum level. The question to ask yourself is, can you offer your goods or services in three or four tiers in order to increase your revenue and your profitability? When clients ordered a wedding photography package from Rachael's company, they could select one of three packages—standard, premier, or elite. Each one of those included more services and would obviously cost more.

Our local neighborhood car wash offers three kinds of car-wash experiences: they have the basic, the deluxe, and the supreme, which are priced respectively at $6.00, $8.00, and $10.00. We would be willing to bet that the majority of consumers do not pick the lowest choice, but probably pick the middle choice. However, if our local car wash only offered one, that's what everyone would pick. Henry Ford said, "You can have any color of Model T Ford you like, as long as it is black." Ford only offered one color.

The other thing that is important to think about is to get over your psychological limitations on pricing. We often talk to entrepreneurs who say no one would ever go for their platinum offering because it's too expensive. Yet they do not know this from trial and error, or from reactions from clients; rather, they have a mindset that people will not pay more money for their products or services. There are many times when people choose to go with Shawn's platinum package, and there are other times they only go for Shawn's gold package.

Make sure not to limit your thinking. People are often willing to invest more money into something they think has tremendous value. Let's face it, that's why there are Mercedes, Lamborghinis, and Maseratis that all seem to sell quite well in the automotive marketplace. What if the people who make Maseratis said, "Gee, no one will ever pay two hundred thousand dollars for a car." But yet every year there are many high-end sports cars sold. Do not limit your thinking; offer three tiers of pricing because you may be surprised at how many people will go for the middle or the top of your pricing tier.

Bundling. Another way of creating tiers for your products or services is to consider bundling. Bundling is taking a series of products and putting them all together into a single package. Let's say you own a travel agency and you sell plane tickets for flights around the world. That is a single product sale. However, if you are bundling you would say you have available a European deluxe package that is bundled to include transportation, airfare, hotel, meals, etc. That would be known as a bundle.

The advantage of a bundle is that people perceive a bundle as being more valuable. Obviously, you also sell more products by bundling because now you're not just selling people plane tickets but you are selling them three or four different items as part of that bundle. Years ago a furniture store in South Florida, Rooms to Go, started offering rooms of furniture as bundles. Instead of selling a single couch, two easy chairs, a coffee table, two end tables, and two lamps separately, the store started selling a living room as one singular package with one price that included all of those items. Shoppers responded positively to this new way of packaging and selling furniture.

SECONDARY SOURCES OF REVENUE

After you have decided on your primary source of revenue, then it is time to think about what other sources of revenue may be beyond your primary source. For example, if you have a firm that designs websites for small to medium-sized businesses, and you have determined that your primary source of revenue is the fee for the design of the websites, then you could possibly add several secondary sources of revenue to your options. Possible sources of secondary revenue could be:

- domains

- search engine optimization (SEO)

- social media management

- website security

Figure out what else you can do that's related or parallel to the goods and services that you already offer in order to increase revenue from a secondary source.

ADD-ON OR UPGRADE

The add-on or upgrade is a way of not increasing primary or secondary sources of revenue, but a way to *add* to revenue in ways that are incremental and seem small but could make a big difference in the overall bottom line of your business. It is why at McDonald's they always ask you if you'd like fries with your hamburger. Whenever we order flowers online, we notice that once the flowers are ordered (primary revenue source), they then offer upgrades, such as adding twelve more flowers for only $4.99, adding a box of chocolates with your order, or upgrading to the deluxe vase for only $10.00 more. These are what most people call upgrades. If a certain percentage of customers go for the upgrades, then a significant amount of revenue could be added to the bottom line.

Think about how you can add upgrades or add-ons in order to make the total sale larger. When Shawn works with a client who is paying him to speak, we often ask if they would like to add a breakout session in the afternoon for a small additional fee (upgrade). Sit down with your team and brainstorm add-ons and upgrades that might be possible for your products, services, and customers.

INTANGIBLES

Another area you may want to consider is an area that most people call intangibles. The tricky part about intangibles is that they do not have a physical form. A product or service is pretty easy for people to understand and easy for them to buy. An intangible, however, is a little more difficult to explain because it does not have a physical form; therefore, it is sometimes harder to sell.

We just rented a car from an online travel site, and after the car was booked they asked if we would like to purchase insurance for the car for the term of our vacation for only $9.00 a day, and the coverage was up to $35,000. Frankly, we were surprised that they were offering it and didn't think about supplemental insurance until they suggested it. This is an intangible. We were renting a car and we knew that the weekly fee we were paying was getting the car, but the intangible add-on was the insurance at $9.00 a day. We can't hold the insurance in our hand, which means it is intangible. But just because something is intangible does not mean that it doesn't have value. What kind of intangibles can you add to your products, goods, and services that may have value to your clients?

One such intangible is *express service*. People could pay extra in order to speed up the manufacturing and/or delivery of the products, goods, or services they are purchasing. As a photographer, every year Rachael would send out postcards in the fall reminding people to get their family Christmas photos taken. Many would get them taken in the fall, but there was always a certain part of the population who waited until the last minute and called in December. They had procrastinated and wanted the photos taken right way. These people could get the express service, but they paid a 100 to 200 percent upcharge.

You could also *offer people insurance* against the loss of their product or service. For example, some companies who specialize in booking vacation travel offer a vacation insurance package that pays for issues that arise from a vacation being delayed or cancelled.

Another intangible is *premium membership*. You could offer your customers a membership and a premium club (for a fee), which would give them certain rights or privileges in their transactions with your company. American Express, for example, charges an annual membership fee for some of their higher end credit cards. People pay the fee in order to experience discounts on special events, early sale of tickets for special events, travel service at no cost, concierge service at no cost, and additional points as part of their loyalty program.

Extended warranties protection or coverage is another great intangible. We are fascinated that almost everywhere we purchase something people ask if we would like to purchase an additional extended warranty. This may be something you want to consider adding to your mix as an intangible. Many people like the psychological comfort of knowing that something has an additional warranty or additional protection and coverage.

When Rachael had her photography business and she contracted to take pictures of someone's wedding, she offered additional wedding photography insurance, which, when purchased, gave them peace of mind to know that if for some reason the photographs did not turn out, or if the film was destroyed or damaged in processing, that there was insurance that would pay (up to $1 million) to have the wedding restaged in order for the photographs to be taken. That gave the brides and grooms a sense of comfort, knowing that they were covered in case anything happened.

CONSULTING

If you are an expert in your field and are selling goods, products, and services, then you may want to offer follow-up consulting in addition to those items.

Here are a few questions to ask yourself when considering adding on products and services in order to increase your primary and secondary revenue sources:

- What *product* can I upgrade?

- What *service* can I upgrade?

- What *product* can I have add-ons for?

- What *service* can I upgrade?

- What *intangible* can I sell?

- What *intangible* can I upgrade?

- What *intangible* can I have add-ons for?

PASSIVE INCOME

Passive income is income that is generated on a passive basis, meaning that you are not actually seeking the income out but you set up a system or process for income to be generated. Wikipedia defines passive income as "an income received on a regular basis with little effort required to maintain it." Examples of passive income could include rental property (where rent comes in each month), interest from bank accounts, dividends from stocks, royalties from publishing, or licensing deals for intellectual property.

You may not believe that your business is a candidate for generating passive income, but certainly you need to have an open mind because it may be possible. For example, if your business designs, manufactures, or invents a product, then you may be able to license the patent or the product to others in different countries. Shawn's publisher, Sound Wisdom, has worked out several arrangements with publishers around the world to publish this series of Jumpstart books, like the one that you are reading right now. Think about passive income that your business could generate.

REVENUE CHANNELS

Let's say that you live in Tuscaloosa, Alabama, and you make some of the world's tastiest pecan pies. Pete's Pecan Pies are the hit of the entire state of Alabama, and people will travel from several states away and take home your pie to family members. This means that Pete's primary source of revenue is having a brick-and-mortar bakery where they are selling Pete's pecan pies. However, there are other distinct possibilities for selling Pete's pies too.

It could be possible that Pete to start selling his pies directly to the consumer through a Pete's pecan pies website. This way Pete's market expands from not only just that part of Alabama, but across the world, providing they can figure out how to ship them without the pies being damaged.

It is entirely possible for Pete to license his pecan pie recipe to a large national distribution company that would sell the pies by geographic territory to grocery store chains. Pete could also sell his recipe to one of the big pie companies, which means they would be sold in the frozen section in grocery stores around the US.

It is also possible that Pete could sign a distribution agreement, where a major food-service distributor will sell Pete's baked pies to restaurants and food-service operations across the country. Pete could make other pies for fast-food chains that people would buy when they bought a burger. They could buy a small version of Pete's pies to have for dessert after they have had their meal.

Pete could also offer other product lines, like packaged pecan pie bars suitable for packing in someone's lunch, cinnamon-roasted pecans in snack bags, and pecan pralines. The list is endless and is limited only by the creativity of each individual entrepreneur.

There are a lot of different ways to sell your product. You could sell your product in a lot of different forms and a lot of different marketing channels to a lot of different audiences. The results are only limited by your thinking. You just have to be creative and think about all of the possibilities. You could have both a retail and a wholesale operation, selling both directly and indirectly. There are many manufacturers who now sell their product to distributors and dealers, while at the same time distributing their product directly to the consumer via the web. It is important to think about all of the different marketing channels for your product, and how each of them could generate either primary or secondary revenue.

Shawn offers full-day and half-day training programs to corporations across the country. They are great customers and we appreciate them very much. However, another interesting fact about Shawn's business is that he also has other training companies that are his clients. They call Shawn, tell him they have a client who wants a session on motivation or leadership, they tell him where the training is located, and want to know if he is available to conduct the training. If he is available they then subcontract to have him conduct training under their brand. The client pays the training company, and the training company pays Shawn. Some of Shawn's clients are corporations, and some of Shawn's clients are other training companies.

In fact, Shawn has revenue from several sources, such as training, speaking, consulting, and licensing. He also offers services in executive coaching, online learning, publishing books, as well as publishing audio programs.

Thinking about your company, products, and services in all of these different ways can be tremendously exciting and motivating because you are expanding your possibilities and your sources of revenue.

> *"The entrepreneur always searches for change,*
> *responds to it, and exploits it as an opportunity."*
> —PETER DRUCKER

WORK IT!

What is your primary source of revenue?

_____

_____

_____

_____

_____

_____

Do you have pricing tiers?

_____

_____

_____

_____

_____

_____

What can be secondary sources of revenue for your business?

_____

_____

_____

_____

_____

What can be incremental revenue for you?

_____

_____

_____

_____

_____

CHAPTER 9

JOLT #8:
USING CREATIVITY IN YOUR BUSINESS

ARE YOU AS CREATIVE AS A FIVE-YEAR-OLD?

"Creativity is just connecting things. When you ask creative people how they did something, they feel a little guilty because they didn't really do it, they just saw something. It seemed obvious to them after a while. That's because they were able to connect experiences they've had and synthesize new things."
—STEVE JOBS

One of the core competencies of growing and/or building a business is the skill of creativity. In today's fast-paced business world, creativity is both required and needed. One of the things that constantly amazes us is the number of people we meet who make statements such as, "I am not creative," "I've never been creative," "You are creative and we aren't," and, "I am not sure that creativity matters that much."

Yet whenever we read stories of successful businesses that are started from nothing—just from a blank piece of paper or rough sketch on the back of a napkin—those stories always contain at least a single spark of creativity.

YOU ARE CREATIVE

How are you able to be creative in your business? The first step is possessing the belief that you indeed are creative and that you have the ability to be creative. In an interesting research project, five-year-olds were given a test to assess their level of creativity. Researchers were shocked to find that 97 percent of the children scored in the highly creative range.

We don't know why they were shocked because we have always found children to be tremendously creative and imaginative. When Shawn's daughter was young, she proudly came into the living room one day and announced she wanted to change her name. When asked what she would wanted to change her name to, she said she would like to change it to Goldenchild Ficarellola. No one to this day knows how she came up with that combination of first and last names, but it certainly was creative to imagine changing your name from Alexis Doyle to Goldenchild Ficarello.

Why are we mentioning this research as it relates to creativity and imagination? Because there is good news hidden within the research. The children who did not score in the highly creative range still scored in the creative range, which means that 100 percent of the children were creative. Why is this important? It is important because that means you were *born creative* and that you have the ability to be creative. The only trick is to know and believe that you are creative, and to tap back into the innate creativity that you already own. You were born with it. You must not believe in the nonsense of people who tell you that you aren't. Your second grade teacher who told you that tree bark could only be colored the approved color of burnt sienna was wrong.

For someone to become more creative, or, as we would describe it, to become creative again, consists of two main steps. First, a person needs exposure in order to be creative. This means you are striving to expose yourself to creative materials and environs in order to retap into your creativity. Second, you need tools. Instead of brainstorming or creating ideas in the old way, you use new tools that help you generate ideas in a more effective and productive way.

EXPOSURE

In order to be more creative and to tap into your innate creativity, you need to strive to increase your exposure to creative ideas and experiences. Here is a list of things you can do in order to increase your level of exposure.

It is important to *do different things*. If you normally go to the same beach every year, during the same month, with the same people, then try to go somewhere different on vacation the following year. When you do things differently, it is extremely stimulating to creativity.

Find out what stimulates your creativity. It may be a certain website, certain periodicals, going to the racetrack, to the movies, or going for a swim, or it could be something like camping or gardening. These are just a few random examples, but the key is to start noting what it is in terms of activity that allows you to be stimulated and more creative.

If you are going to increase your creativity, then you must *train and study for creativity*. As much as it sounds counterintuitive, creative people go to training courses in order to learn how to be even more creative. They study books about creativity to learn all about creativity and brainstorming techniques, and they read biographies of creative people to see what they can glean from their experience. Many people think you can't train yourself to be more creative and that you can't study to be more creative. If that is true, then why are there hundreds of art institutes in the world where artists go to study how to become better artists? There is not just learning to be a better artist from a technical perspective, but it is possible to learn how to be more creative.

Being around creative people will stimulate and inspire your creativity. When you talk to and interact with people who are highly creative, they will challenge and push you to be more creative. You have the innate gift of creativity, but you need to push yourself on a consistent basis in order to grow in your creativity.

Do things that are blatantly creative. You could go to art shows, visit art museums, go to craft shows, go to the theater, to concerts, or to the symphony, or just visit an arts and crafts store. If you have an open mind these activities will most definitely enhance your creativity. Take up some form of art as a hobby, such as poetry, dance, painting, sketching, photography, sculpting, or woodworking.

If you want to stimulate creativity, then *keep a morgue*. A morgue is simply a place you use to collect creative ideas and things that stimulate your creativity. It could be a notebook or file that you physically drop images into from time to time, or things you see in magazines or on the web. You could tear pages out of a catalog, put in a note from a legal pad, a greeting card that someone sent you, a napkin from a restaurant that you wrote on when you were on a business trip, a brochure you liked, or a business card someone handed you.

Rachael had a huge collection of photography books on everything a person could imagine: hand poses, lighting ideas, color ideas, nudes, how to pose people, famous photographers, as well as many others.

She often used these to stimulate her creative thinking. It is possible to also keep an electronic morgue by putting images on Pinterest or some other online storage account like Dropbox or Evernote. When you are involved in coming up with creative ideas, then you simply refer to your morgue in order to stimulate your creativity further.

TOOLS FOR IDEAS

One of the key secrets of coming up with more ideas is to stop using the same old tools that you have always used. Brainstorming is out—people have used brainstorming for far too long and are weary of it. In fact, instead of seeing positive results from it, many are beginning to get negative results from brainstorming. What we would like to do is give you some other tools for coming up with ideas. Here are ten techniques from Shawn's book *Jumpstart Your Creativity.*

Ideation Technique #1: Reverse Brainstorming

Reverse brainstorming is exactly the same as regular brainstorming, except there is a unique twist. Let's say we work for the Billings Bowling Ball Company. We get together with our team in order to brainstorm a way to increase sales and revenue. The objective, as stated, is to "increase sales and revenue."

Instead of brainstorming the old way, we're going to use reverse brainstorming. Instead of talking about how to increase sales and revenue, we will brainstorm a list of the opposite, or the reverse, which is how *not* to increase sales and revenue. This frees up everyone to be highly creative to figure out how *not* to meet the objective. We have conducted this exercise with hundreds of groups, and they always have a lot of fun figuring out ways to mess everything up.

Once several chart pages of ideas have been written down, then we look at all of the ways not to increase sales and revenue, and ask ourselves what the opposite of those would be. This is a highly effective technique for generating a ton of great ideas. We have another name for reverse brainstorming: "What is the dumbest thing you could do?" When we remove the restraint of what can be done, it tends to encourage people's creativity.

Ideation Technique #2: Random Stimulation

Have you ever been riding a bicycle, working out, or taking a shower and come up with a great idea that seemed like it was out of the blue? Sure, all of us have at some point in our lives. We know, however, that the idea was "out of the blue"; rather, it was stimulated by something. It may have been the image on the shampoo bottle, a graphic on the gym wall, or seeing what you saw when riding your bicycle around the marina. It was that spider web/fish net of a brain of yours firing off connections and ideas.

Unconsciously you saw, touched, heard, or felt something that stimulated that idea. This is the phenomenon known as random stimulation. Some outside external stimulus or stimuli randomly triggers your brain to generate an idea. Using this as an ideation technique, we can use one of two approaches to get our brain to randomly generate ideas.

Approach #1. Simply go to Google and click on the Google image tab. Once there, choose various words at random. We might put in *squid* and then look at all the pictures that word generates, then print out one or two images generated by the word *squid*. Then we may pick another word at random, such as *architect*. Pick two images under the architect category and print them out as well. After you go through a series of ten random words and have printed pictures for each of those words, these are used as a random stimulation exercise.

Here's how it would work in a group setting. We would say to the group, "We are currently trying to figure out a way of increasing sales and revenue" (from the bowling ball company example above). Then we ask the group to set that problem aside, and look at a stack of random images. When looking at the images, the group members are only to say what those images remind them of, as a facilitator writes down the phrases and words they mention.

Once a large list of words has been generated from the random photos, you ask the group if any of the words on the list remind them of a solution to the problem. You would be amazed how many times we hear people say, "Oh, that reminds me of something—what if we did this?" The biggest challenge of the random stimulation approach is getting people to believe that a tool that seems completely arbitrary, random, and somewhat abstract is useful in generating ideas.

Though we have seen this approach work many times, we have also seen it not work. The main reason it doesn't work, in most cases, is the fact that the group does not believe the approach will work, so they do not open themselves up to the possibilities, thus shutting down before they start.

Approach #2. This technique is exactly the same as mentioned in number one, but the only difference is the source material for the ideas. In this approach each person brings one or two random magazines or catalogs to the meeting. A person selects a catalog, closes their eyes, and while flipping pages points with their finger to one of the pages. The facilitator then asks what is under their finger, either a word or a picture. The facilitator writes the word or the picture on the flipchart and then follows the same process as outlined above. The key to this approach is making sure there are a variety of magazines from which to choose.

Random stimulation is an effective technique. It has been rumored that this technique has been effectively used for years in Hollywood and New York, in both film and television production. For example, a creative team could sit around and combine different words in order to come up with an idea for a show that was new or different.

Someone could say *Playboy* and *lifeguards*, and of course that would be the television show *Baywatch*. According to sources, that's exactly how the show was pitched to the network, as "Playboy lifeguards."

You could combine two other words, like *millionaire* and *hillbillies*, and come up with the *Beverly Hillbillies*. You could combine *ventriloquist* and *automobile* and come up with the television show *Knight Rider*. We refuse at this point to comment on the mentality of American television, but we're sure you get the idea.

Ideation Technique #3: The Rules

Often we find that organizations have rules in place, which have been in place for a long time. These rules served their purposes well during the time they were enacted, but they may have outgrown their usefulness and may be holding the organization back. The idea behind this technique is to write down a list of all of the rules an organization has (they could be about marketing, sales, design, etc.), and then figure out if those rules were to change, how the ideas would be changed.

For example, we just recently read an article about Applewood Farms, which is an organic meat producer that has grown successfully over the last twenty-five years. One of the defining moments of the CEO's history is when he realized that the company did not have to be in the meat production business. They reworked one of their own rules that said they didn't have to have a manufacturing facility, but they could contract it out. That was a defining moment for the company.

Think of some of the rules that have dominated industries over the past several decades:

- Radio as local (nope).

- Movies are watched at a movie theater (hello, Netflix).

- Books are a physical product (guess again).

- You have to go to college to go to college (wrong).

- Businesses must have a brick-and-mortar presence (laughable).

- Music has a physical from, such as a CD (can you say, download?).

- Data is stored on your computer (hello, the cloud).

- Pizza is cooked in an oven (hi, microwave).

- To find someone to date, you have to go to a club or a church (can you say, eHarmony?).

- You play games on a game system (ha!).

- Yogurt is in a cup (wrong again, GoGurt is in a tube).

Every one of these business opportunities was based on rules and assumptions. If you can make a list of all of your rules and assumptions, and then figure out if they are still relevant and have never been questioned, then you may have the basis of the great idea, or several of them.

Ideation Technique #4: Blank Slate

The idea behind the approach of a blank slate is to remove all restrictions, limitations, and budgets from the ideation process. Come up with an objective, and then say to the group, "If we were starting today from scratch, and had no limitations on structure, finances, and logistics—in other words, if we were starting from a blank piece of paper—how would we handle this problem, challenge, or situation?" When there are no limits, people tend to become a lot more creative and innovative. Once the list is built, then have the group go back and look over the solutions to see if any of them would actually work.

Ideation Technique #5: The Consulting Team

Using this technique, have the group create a list of various celebrities. The celebrities need to be from all areas, including sports, entertainment, literature, and art. Also make sure that they picked both current and past celebrities, including those from history. Once the list is developed, pick a dozen names from the list, which are a mix of both current and past celebrities. Then pose the problem, "How would this problem by handled by Donald Trump? Lady Gaga? Muhammad Ali or Bette Midler? Napoleon, Louis Armstrong, Gustave Eiffel, Renoir, or Thomas Edison? How would it be handled by Mdm. Curie, Hillary Clinton, Ronald Reagan, Big Bird, Donald Duck, or Plato?

The group has a lot of fun coming up with how each celebrity would handle the problem, opportunity, or challenge presented. The best way to do the exercise is to have them go through each celebrity, one at a time, to talk about how they would handle it. Often groups laugh and snicker during this exercise, which seems to border on the edge of being ridiculous at times. But after the list has all been written out as to how each celebrity would handle those situations or problems, the group then goes back to review to see if some of them would make any sense. This can be an effective tool for getting out of your own way and thinking about a problem or situation from a different viewpoint.

Ideation Technique #6: What if This Was?

The idea behind this exercise is to talk about how a problem, opportunity, or challenge would be handled if it was treated as being something else entirely. How does this exercise work? Simply make a list in advance (feel free to use our list below), and then ask the group how they would handle it if it were as described.

For example, let's say we are trying to gain market share from a competitor, so we asked the group, "How would you treat this if it was a war?" The answers are much different than if we say, "How would you handle this if it was a social movement?" It always amazes us how the answers change dramatically when people look at the problem in a completely different and unique way. Here is a suggested list of some of the what-ifs:

- What if it was a war?

- What if it was a movement?

- What if there was an exclusive club?

- What if it was a rare collectible?

- What if it was a party?

- What if it was a dance rave?

- What if it was a celebration?

- What if there was a charitable cause?

- What if it was a patriotic event?

- What if it was an unveiling?

- What if there was a space rocket launch?

- What if it was a visit by state dignitaries?

- What if it was a pep rally?

- What if it was a car show?

- What if it was a football game?

- What if it was a chess match?

Obviously the solutions and ideas from each of these would be remarkable and different. That is the idea and the power of this technique.

Ideation Technique #7: Word Chain

This technique is using words as a way of generating ideas through the technique of word association. Simply put, one person in the group starts with a word and says that word out loud. The next person in the group then has to say a word that reminds them of the previous word. Each word that was spoken out loud needs to be written on a flipchart by the facilitator.

For example, if some says "frog," another person says "hop," then a third person says "beer." Then we end up with a word chain, which is frog, hop, beer, golden, retriever, collector, taxes, Rome, gladiator, fight, gloves, winter, snow, ice, cream, cone, pine tree, floor cleaner, wood, mop, the Beatles, England, the Queen, rock band, etc.

Once that entire list has been written on the chart, the group then goes back and reviews the list of words to see if there is something on that list that could be possibly aligned with, or that would help solve the problem, opportunity, or the challenge the group is faced with.

Ideation Technique #8: Crunchy Cheese Curls

Buy a large bag of crunchy cheese curls and bring them with you to meet with the group. Break the group into smaller groups and then pour a bowl of crunchy cheese curls for each group. Identify the objective that you are working on. Have members of each group pull out a cheese curl, one at a time, and write down what the particular shape of that cheese curl reminds them of. It is important that you purchase crunchy cheese curls and not just the soft kind. The soft kind all have the same shape, whereas the crunchy kind have many unique shapes. It's kind of like looking at the shapes of clouds and imagining what they are. An additional benefit of this exercise is also that you now have snacks as a way to stimulate your creativity.

Ideation Technique #9: Dead Silence

Purchase a bunch of colorful small sticky pads and put them on the table, then state the objective of the ideation and then ask each person to be completely and totally silent for a period of seven minutes. During that time, each person is to write down potential solutions on their three-by-five sticky. When they are done with the seven-minute period of absolute silence, then ask each person to post their sticky notes on the wall, and then review each one, one at a time, in a random order. Generally, we find this exercise to be incredibly helpful as it is rare when people are completely and totally silent. There is often a lot going on when people are trying to ideate.

We have found that we tend to generate great ideas when flying on planes. Our theory is that the reason why planes are so effective is that they are often quiet and we are isolated from interruptions and noises. We have purchased a plane just for the purposes of ideation. Okay, just kidding, we haven't really done that.

Ideation Technique #10: Wacky Hero

Using this technique we get a little crazy and add some humor to the equation by asking a group to have the problem, situation, or challenge solved by a fictitious hero. Once we state the objective, we give the group a list of fictitious heroes and ask them how these heroes would solve the problem. The funny part is that people are both puzzled and fascinated by the names of the heroes, and they have to not only figure out what the hero does (what their superpowers are) but how the hero would theoretically solve the problem.

Here is a list of our fictitious heroes that we use (but hey, this is about creativity, so feel free to make up your own list if you would like). Once people have reviewed each superhero and come up with a list of potential solutions, then they get back together as a group and discuss.

- Butterman

- Green Beany Man

- Blobbo

- Blue Hopper

- Mush Man

- Oil Girl

- Fox Flipper

- Silver Sue

- Waddle Woman

- Trendy Man

- Cloud Rider

- Super Squid

- Underboy

- Mighty Dust Mite

- Wonder Blunder

- Stinger Clown

Give these ten techniques a try. If you would like additional techniques for coming up with ideas, check out Jumpstart Your Creativity for

tons more. Here is a link: http://www.amazon.com/Jumpstart-Your
-Creativity-Jolts-Creative-ebook/dp/B00HK33VX8/ref=tmm
_kin_swatch_0?_encoding=UTF8&sr=1-1&qid=1433175671.

LOOK AT NEW WAYS

Another aspect of creativity is to look at things in new ways,
asking yourself questions like, "What if we did it differently?"
"What if we did it in a new way?" "What if we stopped doing it
the old way?" "What are new ways this is being done in our industry?" Just remember that part of creativity is realizing there is more
than one way to do anything. In order to be creative, you have to
realize that there is not one answer but multiple answers to any
given problem.

DON'T JUDGE IDEAS TOO SOON

We believe that one of the big errors people make as it relates to
creativity is that they try to judge the ideas when coming up with
them. We think, however, that it is a good idea to separate the idea
generation phase and the evaluation phase. In other words, when
you're thinking of ideas you should not be judging them. Once you
have a long list of ideas, then you should set those ideas aside for
a few days before you go through the act of evaluating them. This
will help you be more objective and will not shut down the creative
process either.

When you're able to constantly come up with new, creative, and
innovative ideas, it is stimulating and motivating because you are
moving forward in your business. You are not settling for the old way
of doing things either; rather, you are looking at new ways of doing
things. This is where creativity can be tremendously helpful for you.

"Creativity involves breaking out of established patterns in order to look at things in a different way."
—EDWARD DE BONO

WORK IT!

What is your perception of your own creativity?

_____

_____

_____

_____

_____

_____

_____

What do you need to do to expose yourself to more creative thinking?

_____

_____

_____

_____

_____

_____

What creative thinking tools did you like the most?

_____

_____

_____

_____

_____

_____

Which do you plan on using?

_____

_____

_____

_____

_____

_____

CHAPTER 10

JOLT #9:
MANAGING YOUR THINKING

YOU ARE WHAT YOU THINK...
AND SO IS YOUR BUSINESS

"The essence of optimism is that it takes no account of the present, but it is a source of inspiration, of vitality and hope where others have resigned; it enables a man to hold his head high, to claim the future for himself and not to abandon it to his enemy."
—DIETRICH BONHOEFFER

We believe that your business success is tied directly to the way you think. In order to be successful in starting and running a business, you have to be someone who has the "right" mindset. In this chapter we want to discuss your thinking—specifically, how your thinking has an impact on everything that you do in your professional and personal life. Here are eleven key elements to think about as it relates to the way that you think.

ELEVEN KEY ELEMENTS

Do you think about how you think? In many discussions with people that we have across the country, we realize they have not really thought about how they think. Unfortunately, many people are more in the reactive mode and do things in reaction to events or circumstances. We often see people who are living their lives as if they're flying by the seat of their pants and are never stepping back to analyze and think about how they actually think.

As a business owner and entrepreneur, it is critically important to take a deep dive into thinking about how you think every minute of every hour of every day. Why? Because it affects every decision that you make, how you say everything that you say, how other people react to you, and, we would argue, it will affect your results.

Does your history affect your thinking? There is no question in our minds that the way someone thinks is often based on the context or history of what they've lived. We often hear the saying that "history repeats itself," but that does not have to be true. As human beings we have the ability to change our future by the way we think.

Both of us were fortunate in that we were raised in households by great parents who gave us positive reinforcement and taught us to be optimistic and proactive. Many people we have met, however, were not raised in a household where their parents were positive. In fact, some people were raised in households by parents who were pessimists, or, worse, they were raised by parents who were physically or mentally abusive. But there have also been many people raised in negative environments who overcame it and went on to live successful lives.

The first thing we want you to think about is how your history as a child (or as an adult) affects your current thinking. Do you believe that all things are possible for you, or do you think in a limited way when you think about potential possibilities? Do you believe that just because someone has failed in the past, they're going to fail in the present?

Please take the time to sit down and think about how you think. As far as we know, we are the only species that has this ability. A turtle isn't sitting on a log in the sun thinking about the quality of its life and the quality of its thinking. It is just sitting on a log enjoying the sun.

Here are a few questions to think about in terms of the way you think:

- Do I automatically think more positive thoughts or more negative thoughts? Why is that?

- Do I automatically think about ideas in a big way or in a limited way? Why is that?

- Do I automatically react negatively when people are critical or dismissing of one of my ideas?

- Do I automatically tend to be more reactive or more proactive?

- When faced with a challenge or a problem, do I tend to get frustrated or buckle down and try to solve it?

You'll notice we use the word *automatically* in several of the statements. The idea is to think about what your immediate reaction is when things come up in order to try to modify and change your reactions to those circumstances. Being aware of your automatic reaction and trying to modify it will allow you to develop that skill. Keep in mind that the biggest battle is having an awareness of your reactions so that you can change your thinking. It can be your biggest battle.

Are you thinking big? Are you a big thinker or a limited thinker? Often, when Shawn is traveling around the country, people ask him about the books he has published. They want to know what the titles are, why he wrote them, and how he got them published. What is interesting is that after answering all of those questions, people often say to him that "getting a book published is really hard." What is funny is that Shawn has never thought of the idea that getting a book published is hard, and he has never found getting a book published a difficult task. This is by no means a statement of arrogance or over-confidence, it is just a statement about how he thinks. To be clear: getting a book published *is hard*, but if you think it's hard then it becomes a truth for you and you act differently.

Oftentimes in life, when we think something is going to be hard, it is, and if we think something is going to be limited, we often limit it. So our thinking, if it is in the limited mode, will limit our progress; but if we are thinking expansively and thinking big, then it will expand our progress. Do you believe your business can do $1 million in revenue? Do you believe your business can do $10 million in revenue? Do you believe your business can do $100 million in revenue? As you read through these questions, what was your reaction to each of the questions? How you reacted to these questions will say a lot about how you think.

Also, thinking big is exciting, motivating, and it attracts you to opportunities in the world because you are positive, upbeat, and motivated. If you think big, it impacts your actions, and your actions impact your results.

Do you think you have the right? Many people we meet as we travel around the country ask questions like, "What gives me the right to start a business?" or, "How can I start a business if I do not have enough talent?" So one of the areas of thinking that you may want to consider is, do you think negatively about yourself and think you may not have the right to have a successful business? This can also be a function of low self-esteem or a lack of confidence.

We are sure you know what we would have to say about that: "What do you mean you do not have the right to start a business?" Well, in answer to that we say of course you have the right! That is what makes the world a wonderful place—you have opportunities to build a business if you so choose, and you have the freedom to create whatever it is that you want. Walt Disney can build Disneyland, Mary Kay can start a cosmetics company, and Ben Carson can become a world-famous neurosurgeon and presidential candidate. Did Walt and Mary Kay and Ben have the right to do what they did? Or course they did. But even if they didn't have the right, they did it anyway.

You have the right too. If you are willing to work hard and have a great idea, service, or product, then why not you? Do other people deserve it more than you do? Are they smarter? No, of course not. Are they more talented? Not necessarily. You have to say to yourself that you are smart, you are talented, you have a good idea, you have the right to own a business, and yes, you can become a multimillionaire if you are willing to work hard enough.

If you have the feeling like you have not earned the right, then you need to continually work on changing those thoughts by saying to yourself that you do have the right and you have earned it. Associate with people who are positive, upbeat, and optimistic. Then people who believe in you and will tell you so and that will help you feel better about yourself and your right to build an empire. Own it. Claim it.

Are you committed in your thinking? When you think about how you think, then you think about how committed you are to building and running your business. Are you 1,000 percent committed? Are you buying or renting your business? People who are renting are not committed; they're just renting for a limited amount of time. They are not "all in." The people who are buying are completely and fully committed. Are you willing to do what it takes? Are you willing to work nights and weekends and long hours in order to build your business? In terms of your thinking, it takes 1,000 percent commitment. We are working on the final edits of this book at one in the morning on July 4. We are committed.

What do you think about your ego? Some people are confused about the difference between being confident and being egotistical. Many people believe they are the same, but we believe there is a huge difference between the two. We are not saying that you should be an egotistical maniac, but what we are saying is that you should be confident. Own your greatness. Jen Sincero said in the title of her book, *You Are a Badass*—believe it, because you are.

Unfortunately, while being raised many people are told by parents and other well-meaning people in authority not to be overly confident. They say things like, "Don't be egotistical," and, "Don't get a big head," and, "Don't brag." These parents and authority figures are well-intentioned—they're trying to raise a person who is not a sociopath and who does care about others. They're also trying to raise someone who is empathetic and helpful. These are all good; however, the impact of hearing these types of statements throughout your formative years is that you tend to limit the way you think because you don't want to be "too egotistical." This is like putting your foot on the brakes on a racecar. You are saying, "I can do this; I'm great at it," while your conditioned mindset is saying, "I don't know, that kind of sounds like bragging to me." Be careful of this kind of thinking.

In order to be successful in business, you have to be confident. Why? Well, it's obvious that you have to believe in what you're doing in order to start a business where a paycheck is not guaranteed. You have to be confident and willing to accept the risks, for that takes a great deal of confidence in your abilities and your skills. Just be careful and do not allow the people in your past or your present to dissuade you from your gifts. There is nothing wrong with having a healthy ego and feeling good about your skills and abilities. You are great.

Is your thinking proactive? The dictionary defines *proactive* as "serving to prepare for, intervene in, or control an expected occurrence or situation, especially a negative or difficult one; anticipatory." The question is, do you think in a proactive way? Are you preparing for what may happen in your business? Or to control situations? It is always better to be proactive than reactive, because you get ahead of the curve in your business when you're proactive.

We have always been amazed that certain businesses don't see certain trends coming because they're not proactive. For years Blockbuster kept hearing about Netflix and the trend of streaming video, but they were not proactive about it. They didn't consider it to be a threat to their business. Because they were not proactive in seeing what was around the corner, all of their stores ended up going out of business because people simply stopped driving to the store to get a video.

In the South they used to have a saying: "Let sleeping dogs lie." The thought behind that saying is that you are only to react if the dog wakes up. The new way of proactive thinking is to go over gently and wake up the dog before it has a chance to wake up when you least expect it.

Whenever Shawn does live training or speaking, he always makes sure to have a plan B. For example, if each participant for a half-day training program is supposed to get a handout, Shawn brings one copy of his own so that if for some reason the handouts are not available, then the client could make a copy of Shawn's file so that everyone can have a handout. So plan B is really being a proactive thinker because you're preparing for things that could possibly go wrong. When Rachael took photos as a professional photographer, she always had tons of extra film, cameras, and battery packs. If one piece of equipment failed, she had several camera backups.

Is your thinking resilient? When you start or run a business, there are going to be times when things do not go as planned, and there may be times when sales are down, or an employee quits. Now is the time to figure out before that happens whether or not you are able to think in a resilient way. People who succeed in business do not allow their thinking to be swayed by negative events and people. Can you man the helm during a storm and stay the course? Will you keep holding on to the wheel as you are being hit by each wave? If so, what would be the tools you would need to do so?

There will be people who will give you negative feedback, people who will criticize your work and your company, and people who will tell you all the reasons why it will not work. These are people you need to ignore, not letting them affect your confidence in your business or in your own abilities.

We recently read a story about Giorgio Armani, the famous fashion designer. In the article it said that he did not accomplish anything or launch his own line until he was in his mid-forties. He was a medical student who did not become a doctor; rather, he was making his living doing window dressing for a department store. He eventually got promoted, becoming the menswear buyer, and after that he became a designer. Had Giorgio not had resilience in his thinking, then he would've given up and never launched his fashion line. Today his fortune is calculated at being somewhere near $7 billion.

We often wonder how many people faced adversity and gave up when they were right on the edge of success. Maybe they would have succeeded had they been more resilient in their thinking. I am sure you have heard the story of R. U. Harby, as outlined in the book *Think and Grow Rich.* Harby worked with his uncle who had found a vein of gold ore. His uncle had raised money for all the machinery, and they were excited they were mining gold. It was going so well they had paid off all their debts. Then, suddenly, no gold. The gold just seemed to run out. They finally gave up and sold the machinery to a junkyard and went home. The junkman hired a mining engineer to take a look. The mining engineer discovered there was more gold. It was three feet away from where Harby and his uncle stopped digging. Just three feet.

Do you shape your thinking by being inspired by others? It is a good idea to shape your thinking by being inspired by others, either by reading books about successful people, by working with mentors, or by watching documentaries about successful people. Whether it's an article in a magazine, the *Wall Street Journal,* or a video online, seeing how other businesspeople have succeeded can be inspirational and motivational, but it can also help shape your thinking. It's almost as if you're borrowing thinking methodologies from the people you read about and admire. Maybe you soak up some of Steve Jobs's fearless thinking as it relates to business (Apple), maybe you soak up some of Ed Cantmull's thinking as it relates to creativity (Pixar), maybe you pick up some of Mark Zuckerberg's thinking as it relates to technology (Facebook), or maybe some of Indra Nooyi's ideas about running a big business (Pepsi). Or maybe you borrow some thinking from some of John H. Johnson's ideas about how to build a publishing empire (Johnson publishing).

By reading, watching, and studying about other people's lives, you can take valuable lessons and use them to shape your own thinking. You can say to yourself, "Well, that is really interesting. How can I use that process to help me in my business?" Make a list of all the people you find interesting in the world of business—some of your "business heroes"—and start reading, watching, and studying about them. Rachael was always inspired by the work of Monte Zucker, who was a successful wedding photographer. See what kernels of inspiration, motivation, and thought processes you can extract from their lives.

Do you improve your thinking by journaling? We are not suggesting you sit down every night and write exactly what happened every single day in your journal, but there's absolutely incontrovertible evidence that indicates that people who are great thinkers are often writing down their ideas in a journal or book and going back and reviewing those thoughts over time. Leonardo da Vinci, John Adams, Lewis Carroll, Marie Curie, F. Scott Fitzgerald, Buckminster Fuller, and Harry Truman were all famous for journaling.

Writing down your thoughts makes them more tangible and allows you to examine them in a deeper way. Furthermore, if you write down a thought and it is recorded on paper, that thought is in essence harvested for your use at a future time. That way you can go back and look at it a year or two later. Even when the thought has already been forgotten, it still exists on paper in your archives. And you say, "Oh, I forgot about that idea—that was a good one." Having your ideas in writing may also help you stimulate new ideas for the future. It is a manual way of thinking about how you think. In fact, some experts on creativity also call this displayed thinking, which we think is a good way to describe it. You are displaying your thinking.

Do you practice reinvention thinking? The human brain is capable of many things. And one of the things that is possible for you is to reinvent yourself, your business, and your life—really, anything you put your mind to. With thinking and creativity, anyone has the capability of being the architect of his or her own life. It is a shame that some people think this is not realistic or true. However, we have seen many people who have decided to change their life just by thinking about it and taking action.

A great example of this idea is one of our fellow Sound Wisdom authors, Kimanzi Constable. He was delivering bread in the freezing weather of Wisconsin, hating both his life and his job. He decided to become a book author and professional speaker, and after a family vacation to Hawaii decided that his family would eventually live in Hawaii. He then wrote and published a very successful book, *Are You Living or Existing?* He built his speaking and coaching empire, and he now lives with his family in Hawaii. This is a great example of a man who practiced reinvention thinking. Are you willing to practice the fine art of reinvention thinking? These are some thought processes that you need be continually aware of, and it will help you if you carefully think about and consider each one.

WORDS MATTER

If you want to adjust your thinking, then you'll also need to adjust your language. Something that can be helpful here is to talk as much as possible in the positive. Instead of saying, "I hope I have a good month next month," say instead, "I'm going to have a great month next month." Instead of saying, "I sure hope this product is going to be a best seller," say instead, "This product is going to be a best seller."

All we are doing is replacing some of the words, such as "hope" with "going to," because the idea is to make your words a self-fulfilling prophecy. For example, if you work you can say, "Boy, I sure hope they don't fire me," or you can say, "I'm doing such a great job. They are going to have to promote me." Over the next several weeks, we challenge you to listen carefully to the words you use, because the words you use affect your thinking. Your thinking affects your words, which, in turn, affect your thinking; your words affect your actions too. This particularly applies to negative words, so avoid them at all costs.

We hear people say words like these all the time: can't, won't, shouldn't, never, impossible, won't work, didn't, wouldn't, couldn't, will not, no, but, and weird. Often, when coaching business clients, they will say to us, "Well, that's a good idea, but I can't possibly generate revenue to the levels that you're describing—it's just impossible." What this person has done is eliminate all possibilities of succeeding because it has been decided by their way of thinking in advance that it is not going to work. It is indeed a self-fulfilling prophecy. Change your language, change your thinking, and you will change your life. Then make sure the people you work with also are speaking in the positive and speaking positive words, not negative ones.

LIMITS

We hear people say that sometimes certain things are not possible. Shawn's father, Jack, often says that people put fences around themselves, then they blame others for building them. We believe this to be true. Most limits are self-installed and are therefore reinforced by them being repeated over and over. Limits can take several forms.

Limit of self. This is where the person lacks confidence in themselves and puts limits on their own capability. People with this belief say things like, "I could never do something like that," or, "I'm too shy," or, "I'm not smart enough," or, "I'm not tall enough," or, "I'm not skinny enough," or, "I'm not something enough." Stop it! The only limits you have are the ones you place on yourself. Yes, that is correct: these limits are self-imposed.

Limit of resources. People with this limiting belief believe there's not enough to go around. They will say things like, "I can never afford that," "I don't have enough money," "That is too expensive," "We can never sell something for that," or, "I can't afford the inventory." Some limits of resources may actually be true, but we find that people who lack resources can truly be the most creative and can come up with some pretty amazing solutions.

Limits of the system. These are people who say, "Oh, there are rules about that," "They will never let us do it that way," or, "The city, state, or federal government will not let me do it that way." By the way, these people often answer that way when they are assuming, because many times they have never checked with the city, the state, or the government to see if it's really true.

We are sure you have heard of an American company called Uber. The company was founded in 2009 by Garrett Camp and Travis Kalanick. Uber technology gives consumers the ability to press a button on their phone and submit a trip request, then a private car picks them up and takes them where they need to go (we actually use this service all the time). If Garrett or Travis would've believed in the limits of the system, then they would have believed that what they were doing was illegal because many municipalities claimed you could not pick people up unless you had a taxi license. Many governments and taxi companies have protested against their company, but it has been successful—it's been estimated that the company will generate $10 billion in revenue by the end of 2015. They did not believe in the limits of the system.

YOU ARE WHAT YOU THINK

For about the last 120 years, authors have been writing about the concept known as the law of attraction. This concept was originally written about by people like Prentice Mulford, who wrote a book called *Thoughts Are Things*, and James Allen, who wrote a book called *As a Man Thinketh,* and Wallace D. Wattles, who wrote a book called *The Science of Getting Rich.* Of course, the most popular author who wrote about this concept is Napoleon Hill in his book

Think and Grow Rich, which was published in 1937. And in recent history, this concept has been made popular through a book called *The Secret* by Rhonda Byrne.

What is this concept that is so important? It is the concept of the law of attraction. The basic concept behind the law of attraction is that you attract what you think about the most. It's the concept of like attracts like. Probably the best analogy that we have seen to describe the law of attraction is that your mind is like a signal tower, and the signals that you send out attract back similar signals. Before you run screaming from the room, thinking we are going to drop some strange pseudo-scientific New Age claptrap on you, please give this concept careful consideration.

Many of us growing up have heard the term "you are what you think," and we believe to a large extent that it is true. What are some key concepts from the law of attraction that you can use in order to modify, adapt, and change your way of thinking in order to get better results? Here are some ideas.

Thinking matters. The entire idea behind the law of attraction is that thoughts are energy, and the energy we use when we think is like a magnet: our thoughts draw to us either positive or negative things and people. I'm sure you have heard the term birds of a feather flock together, that's kind of how the law of attraction works. As this simple description goes "like attracts like." The world is made up of energy, and your energy affects the energy of everything and everyone else. That sounds complicated in a way, and it is, but just think of it this way: if you think positively, then you get positive results; however, if you think negatively, then you'll most likely get negative results.

We have all met people who say things like, "Nothing good ever happens to me," and, "I always have bad luck," or, "I never win anything." This is both a self-fulfilling prophecy and it is the theory of the law of attraction. In essence, they think they are attracting bad luck. When you are thinking, try to make sure you are trying to eliminate negative thoughts and focusing on positive thoughts instead.

Control your emotions. Make sure that you control your emotions in a positive way, because one of the key concepts behind the law of attraction is not only do positive thoughts attract positive actions, but when positive emotion is applied, it enhances and amplifies the power of the law of attraction. The idea is that positive thinking and positive emotions draw in positive experiences and results; likewise, negative emotions and negative thoughts draw in negative experiences and results.

Free will. Another concept behind the law of attraction is the idea that when we have a thought about any given topic, we are creating something new. When we freely choose to be the architects of our own lives, and we think new thoughts and new ideas, then those new thoughts and ideas will attract similar ones into our life. Think of it as a form of free will. Free will allows you to make a choice about what to think about, and when you think about what you choose to create, it attracts other people who think along the same lines.

Focus. Another key concept behind the law of attraction is that you get whatever it is that you're focusing on. Be sure you focus on what you want and don't allow any room for doubt and focus. If you focus on what you want in a positive dynamic, then you're more likely to get it. If you're focusing on what you don't want, then you're more likely to get exactly that as well. So use your energy and your time focusing on positive desires rather than negative ones.

Action. An interesting idea from the law of attraction basically says that everything you have and everything that you do is a result of prior thoughts. Taking that a step further, the law of attraction states that every positive or negative event that happens in your life was attracted by you. But it can also be used backward: we think about something and take action, then the law of attraction says that this is different, and all *action is a result of prior thoughts*. This one is hard for people to understand, that what you think about determines your future actions. Obviously, then, it becomes important to control your thinking.

Change. We believe if you want to change your life, the first and most important thing that you have to do is change your thinking. The law of attraction states that when you have a thought, you create a vibration, and that vibration affects everyone and everything around you. That means if you want to change the way your life and your business are going, then alter your thoughts.

Belief. What is belief? Belief is a long-standing pattern of thinking. These patterns of thinking could have been formed as you were growing up, and they were probably influenced by people who raised you, such as your parents, authority figures, and teachers. Or they could be beliefs you've developed as an adult, which are based on experiences, observations, or through your learning.

Another way experts describe a belief is something known as a meme. A *meme* is simply an accepted way of thinking about something that takes traction in our society, and everyone then believes it. For example, people may say most artists are eccentric. This is a meme people have come to accept about all artists. The reality is that, however, you cannot apply a singular label to a group of people that have a population in the millions.

The problem with both your beliefs and memes that you've accepted as truth is that they may or may not be true. And even more damaging than that, they may actually hurt you in building your business and managing your life. Often we hear people say most businesses fail within the first five years, which is true. When both of us started our businesses, the last thing we wanted to focus on was the idea that most businesses fail in the first five years. Both of us said to ourselves that failure was not an option. Just because something is true does not mean it has to be your truth.

Part of the law of attraction says that you need to deeply examine your beliefs to make sure they are not causing issues and problems with your business and your life. If your beliefs are negative, or focusing on what you don't want, then you need to reevaluate and change your beliefs in order to get better results.

Gratitude. Sit down and take some time to write out what most experts call a gratitude list. What is a gratitude list? It is simply a list of all the things that you're grateful for in your life, both personally and professionally. You may be grateful for the beautiful home that you live in, your wonderful wife, your amazing husband, your good health, your children, for specific talents that you have been given, for having a great business, or for your irritating poodle.

The basic concept about gratitude in the law of attraction is that when you express gratitude for what you have been given, then you create an energy that attracts more to you because you're grateful for what you already have. Most law-of-attraction experts say that having gratitude will allow you to manifest more.

The main thing we want you to do is to focus on how you think and to make adjustments where adjustments need to be made. When planes are flying, they constantly get off course and the pilot is always readjusting to keep the plane on course. You need to do the same thing with your thinking. Almost all of the successful people we know and have met in our lives have been absolute masters at controlling their thinking, because they realize their thinking is such a huge impact on their life, both personally and professionally.

"Don't ever criticize yourself. Don't go around all day long thinking, "I'm unattractive, I'm slow, I'm not as smart as my brother." God wasn't having a bad day when he made you.... If you don't love yourself in the right way, you can't love your neighbor. You can't be as good as you are supposed to be."
—JOEL OSTEEN

WORK IT!

Do you think about how you think? When? How often?

_____

_____

_____

_____

_____

_____

_____

How does your history affect your thinking?

_____

_____

_____

_____

_____

_____

Are you thinking big? If not, then why?

_____

_____

_____

_____

_____

How do you gain inspiration from other people? What can you do more?

_____

_____

_____

_____

_____

Do you practice law-of-attraction thinking?

_____

_____

_____

_____

_____

CHAPTER 11

JOLT #10:
KEEP GROWING

IF YOU ARE NOT GROWING,
YOU ARE SLOWING

Since this book is about getting and staying motivated while starting or running a business, then we passionately believe that you have to keep learning and growing. In Shawn's book, *Jumpstart Your Motivation*, he dedicated an entire chapter to being a nonstop, continuous learning machine. This gives you a competitive advantage, which is an important way to keep stimulated and motivated as you embrace the challenge of running or starting a business.

In order to continue your development as a business professional, you need to embrace learning.

TRAINING TO BE THE BEST YOU CAN BE

We think that it is unfortunate that most people across the world, upon graduating from high school or college, deliberately stop learning, erroneously think that they are done with their education.

The irony is that the commencement ceremony, which is part of graduation, contains the word *commencement*. If you look up *commencement*, it doesn't mean to stop; rather, it means to begin. When people stop learning, they lose motivation and get stagnant. Therefore, you must keep learning.

What is learning? The dictionary defines *learning* as to gain knowledge, comprehension, or mastery through experience or study. In order to be successful in business, you must have many different skill sets and a broad base of knowledge. To run a successful business, you'll need leadership ability, selling skills, problem-solving skills, marketing, publicity, logistics, accounting, communication skills, emotional intelligence, creativity, great customer service, psychology, interviewing skills, intelligence, or industry-specific knowledge. You may also need a tolerance for risk, energy, sensitivity, planning, negotiating, and management skills. And those are just a few of the possible skills you may need to successfully start and run a business.

What you need to do, however, is go through a list similar to the one above and decide what your areas of strength are and what areas you need improvement. Next, what you'll need to do is to come up with some sort of action plan to receive training in those particular areas. Then the question arises, how do you get this information for training in those areas?

FINDING WHAT YOU NEED

Once you've decided what areas you need training in, the next phase is to find out where you can receive training. You will find several resources in chapter 4 that you may be able to tap into in order to get trained in a particular topic. But here are some other ideas regarding training that you may want to consider.

Udemy. This is one of the best sources for online training. At the time of this writing, they have over 8,000 courses and 3 million users who sign in and take courses, either for free or for a small fee. What is great about Udemy is that you can take the courses in your time, and they actually mark where you have stopped so you can start and stop the program whenever you like. Each program contains videos (by subject-matter experts), audios, power points, and handouts.

Udemy has tremendous quality assurance, and the programs are well-designed. Shawn has many programs on Udemy, one is Jumpstart Your Presentation Skills and another called The 30 Day Motivational Makeover. The programs have thousands of students. Take a look at this site to see if you can find what you need in order to get training.

Local colleges. There are many great local community and four-year colleges that offer noncredit programs or for-credit programs. Most of them also offer training programs on a regular basis. One of our local community colleges sends out a catalog every quarter that lists the hundreds of training programs they offer, each one lasting only about three months. See if you can tap into some of these as a resource. Additionally, many of them also offer online training.

Professional coaching. A big trend right now in the world of business is for entrepreneurs to hire their own life coach or professional skills coach. Shawn, for example, is a certified executive coach, and Rachael and Shawn coach people one-on-one by phone, by Skype, or in person. The advantage of using a professional coach is that you get someone who is specially trained, an individual who has a lot of experience, and one who has a lot of tools and assessments to help you evaluate where you are and where you need to be. The other great advantage of a professional coach is that they offer an outside objective opinion. Professional coaches charge a wide array of fees that are often worth the investment in terms of getting where you need to go.

Outside training companies. There are several companies that travel around the country and offer individual one-day or two-day seminars on a given topic, whether it is leadership, creativity, organizational skills, or communication skills. Keep an eye out for these touring companies and see if you can attend one of these seminars when they are close by. They often offer decent quality courses and good facilitators, all at a reasonable price.

Company resources. If you have started your own company on the side, working only part time, and you are still working for a company full time, then talk to someone in your human resources department to see what training resources they have available to help you. Many corporations have a vast array of training programs, both online and live, that you can sign up for at no cost to you.

TED talks or TEDx. At the time of this writing, a search of the TED talks site (www.TEDtalks.com) reveals that there are over 1,900 talks you can watch, all of them delivered by world-class expert speakers in videotape presentations. They are filmed in front of a live audience, most of them somewhere between twelve and eighteen minutes long. There are 30,000 more videos on the TEDx talks site, which are the result of independently produced TEDx meetings around the world. These are also extremely high quality. All of these videos can be searched by topic and watched absolutely free.

Associations. Find out what the appropriate associations are for your industry, and find out if they have both local and/or national meetings. For example, when Shawn first got into the training industry, he found out about the American Society of Training and Development. As it turns out, the association had both local chapter meetings and a national meeting once a year. What was offered at the local and the national meetings were training programs on every imaginable topic related to training and employee development.

Associations can be a rich resource for training programs, materials, and workbooks.

Google. By looking for a particular topic on Google, you may find a tremendous amount of resources that are available to you for a small fee or for nothing at all. Once you enter in a Google search, it will show you white papers, research, books, video presentations, and audios—an entire range of materials that relate to your topic. This can be a helpful resource for locating training materials.

Libraries. This sounds like a lame and old-fashioned recommendation, but believe us when we say that it is not. Many libraries in the new world have modernized and caught up with technology. Many of them now offer ongoing programs, online learning programs, book downloads for your Kindle, Nook, or iPad, and a large collection of nonfiction videos and audios. We are not sure if you remember, but you can also get physical books there too. In most communities a library card is no charge at all.

The chamber of commerce. We have been impressed with how far chambers of commerce have come in the last several years. They are no longer your dad's old-fashioned chambers of commerce. Rather, many local chambers of commerce offer single- and multiple-day training programs, they offer the ability for companies to tap into local and federal grants for training, and they offer affinity groups, such as groups for mentoring women and minorities. They also offer many other services, which you may find surprising. Check out your local chamber of commerce to see what resources are available to help you get the training you need.

YouTube. We are constantly amazed at the depth, breadth, and quality of videos that are available on YouTube. Search for any topic and you will be amazed to find thousands of videos on that topic, many of them produced and created by subject-matter experts. The other great advantage of YouTube is that once you find a subject-matter expert who has good content, you can subscribe to their YouTube channel. Then, each time they come out with a new offering, you will receive a message saying they have posted a new video. For example, a search on the term "negotiating skills" resulted in 63,800 results. Some of the videos are only ninety seconds long, and some of them are as long as an hour and fifteen minutes. And all of the videos appear to be free.

Ask others. Another interesting technique is to ask other colleagues, partners, and vendors if they know of training resources available on a particular topic that you're looking for. Often, people you know already have identified and worked with a company that provided training exactly around what it is that you're looking for. Asking someone else can save you a lot of time. Take recommendations from others who have experienced the training.

READING/STUDYING

In addition to attending training programs, reading can be a tremendous resource to help you learn more about any topic that you're interested in. The great thing about reading is that the world is so full of rich resources for your use, helping you learn what you need to know. Here are some ideas about how to locate reading materials you may find helpful.

Books. A quick search on Amazon or Google will tell you books that are available in the subject matter that you're looking for, as well as give you helpful reviews that may guide you in making your decisions about what books to purchase and read. The great thing about new technology with book readers, such as the Kindle and the Nook, is that you can save time by instantly downloading a book with a press of one button, and your materials can be archived in your library contained within your device or on the cloud so you can refer back to those materials anytime you desire. We find often that many of the books we have located for our Kindles we could not have found in a traditional bookstore, because traditional bookstores can't carry that depth of inventory. You have to decide whether you want to own a physical book or just get a book as a download. Obviously, there are positives and negatives of each.

Online articles. There are so many great websites that have good articles you can download and read for free. Often, just by doing a Google search on a particular topic, you can find many articles that give you the information that you need in a fairly quick manner. You can then either download the article or print it out and read it. The fact that these articles are available at your fingertips is a huge advantage because you can start learning instead of having to wait. The other advantage is that the cost of acquiring knowledge has gone down dramatically in the last several years, so knowledge is inexpensive.

Magazines. It can give you a competitive advantage in business by subscribing to magazines, either physically or electronically. Most magazines now offer both options, to either download a magazine onto your iPad, your Kindle, or some other electronic device, or to receive a physical magazine in the mail. The great thing about magazines is that they can give you great ideas, tips, and tools without taking up a huge amount of your time if you're a busy person.

Some of our favorite business magazines we subscribe to and like to read are *Success, Fast Company, Forbes, Fortune, Wired, Entrepreneur, Inc., Real Simple,* and *Psychology Today.* Those are a few periodicals you might want to consider subscribing to. The good news is that these days subscriptions have gone way down in price and many magazine publishers are offering special deals.

Newspapers. There are basically three kinds of newspapers you may want to consider reading. First are national newspapers, like the *Wall Street Journal* or the *New York Times.* The second kind of newspaper is what we call a business newspaper. For example, in our area there is a magazine called *Business 2 Business*. This periodical features good articles, many tips, tools, and techniques relating to the world of business, as well as local business-related stories. These help you keep up with the local business community and also help you learn more about the latest and greatest business practices. The third kind of newspaper is your local community newspaper, which in our area would be the *Philadelphia Inquirer*. The local newspaper may not help you learn anything new about business skills, but it can keep you informed as to what's going on in your community and the local business community, because these newspapers often have a business section.

Audio programs. If you are a busy person (and who isn't these days?), then another way to squeeze in your reading time is to download audio versions of the books you want to read. You can then listen to your books when you are working out at the gym, riding your bike, or doing housework. This is a great way to educate yourself and increase your efficiency in terms of time management.

There are also now several online programs that allow you to pay a monthly fee of around $15.00 (like audible.com), and you can listen to an unlimited amount of books. A quick look at Audible and we found 8,600 nonfiction titles. We also meet people who just don't like to read, and so the audiobook may be a good alternative for them. Many of our books are available in audio versions as well, of which many people tell us they greatly appreciate.

Self-study courses. There are also many self-study courses available for purchase online, either as a download or as a physical program, with binders and audios. These courses are not taken online, but are taken on your own through the use of various workbooks. They are designed to help you study a particular topic over a defined amount of time, and they can be helpful and a good value based on the purchase price.

EXPERIENCE

Another great way to learn is to create opportunities to experience the very thing that you want to learn about. Here are some ways you can learn about your respective area by creating experiences where you get hands-on learning.

Apprentice. When Shawn first got into training, he joined a company's training department without having any experience in training. Because he wanted to learn, he started at the bottom rung of the ladder, but in nine years he learned a lot and was able to write, design, develop, implement, and facilitate over a hundred training programs. This was the best kind of apprenticeship anyone could have. Likewise, when Rachael first wanted to become a professional photographer, after studying and learning, she became a photographer's assistant, helping them do photo shoots at weddings, as well as helping out on some commercial shoots. Later in her career she had young assistants working with her so they could learn the business too. By watching, observing, and participating in photo shoots, she learned a great deal. If you want to learn more, then figure out how you can become an apprentice in order to learn the industry.

Volunteer. If you want to learn leadership skills, for example, volunteer to serve in a leadership role in a local civic, charitable, or religious organization. By serving in a leadership role, you will learn a great deal about how to manage and lead groups of people and projects.

Work for free. Shawn has met several people who are aspiring professional speakers, and when they ask for advice on how to break into the professional speaking industry, the advice that Shawn gives them is to speak. When they ask what that means, he tells them to go and find organizations that are looking for speakers at their meetings and volunteer to do it for free. This way they get to practice their skills, develop their keynote topics, and build a list of clientele, all while getting great experience.

Les Brown, the famous motivational speaker and author, wanted to be in the radio business as a DJ when he was young. No station would hire him as an on-air DJ, so he finally got permission to work at a local radio station for free. He would come and serve coffee, sweep the floors, and do whatever else that needed to be done, never making a nickel for his work. However, one fateful night one of the DJs got drunk on the air and was not able to continue his program. Because Les had a ton of experience watching, observing, and practicing, he was able to immediately jump in and take over the DJ's radio show. He did such a good job they hired him to actually be a DJ with his own radio show.

Toastmasters. You may not be familiar with Toastmasters, but it is an organization that specializes in helping people develop skills, such as speaking skills, leading and facilitating a meeting, communication skills, and impromptu speaking skills. The greatest aspect of Toastmasters is that once you join you then have the ability to go to meetings and serve different roles. You get to experience speaking and receiving feedback, running meetings as the Toastmaster, experiencing the challenges of leading a meeting, and getting to serve various other roles. The beauty of Toastmasters is that you get exactly what it is you're looking for—experience. Shawn participated in two different kinds of Toastmasters clubs and learned a great deal from those experiences. He was also able to compete in the world championship of speaking, which was a fun experience as well.

If you're interested in Toastmasters, just go to www.Toastmasters .org to see if there is a chapter located near you. In many towns, there are multiple chapters, some of which meet in the mornings, some that meet at lunchtime, and some that meet in the evening hours. Membership is extremely reasonable in terms of cost, the main cost being your investment of time in preparing for and attending the meetings. You may think that Toastmasters has nothing to do with being an entrepreneur, but it is about being an effective communicator. When you have the chance to speak, present, and run meetings, you'll want to be able to hit it out of the park.

Part-time work. Another way of getting experience in your field and learning more is to have a full-time job that pays the bills and do a part-time job that helps you learn what it is that you're trying to learn. This gives you valuable experience that cannot be gained any other way. See if there may be a part-time job available in a field for you to start learning more about, then see if you can fit it into your schedule.

Ride along. If none of the above techniques work and no one will give you a chance to apprentice or work part time, you can ask for permission to ride along with them as they do their work. For example, some people who aspire to be police officers will get permission from the police department to ride with an officer for his or her entire shift. This way they learn a great deal by observing and seeing what real police work looks like on a daily basis. This also gives the person who's riding along a realistic version of what the work is, as opposed to the "Hollywood glamour" version that is often presented on television.

MAKE UP YOUR MIND

Make up your mind on what it is that you want to learn, what it is you need training in, and what it is that you need to experience. Once you have made those decisions, then you need to create an individual development plan and turn it into action, not letting anyone tell you that you can't do it.

If you become a nonstop learning machine, then you'll be well ahead of the game. Learning your industry and skill sets are vital to becoming successful. The world of business today is a fast-paced, dog-eat-dog, competitive, and sometimes brutal environment. It is up to you to decide how you're going to get and stay motivated as you start to manage and run a company.

If you are really determined and are willing to work hard and have the right mindset and attitude, then the world can truly be your oyster. Racecar driver Mario Andretti once said, "Desire is the key to motivation, but it's determination and commitment to an unrelenting pursuit of your goal—a commitment to excellence—that will enable you to attain the success you seek."

WORK IT!

What skills do you need to work on? Why?

_____

_____

_____

_____

_____

_____

What are some of the sources where you can go to get this training?

_____

_____

_____

_____

_____

_____

What are some books you want or need to read?

_____

_____

_____

_____

_____

_____

What are some experiences that would help you learn?

_____

_____

_____

_____

_____

_____

_____

CHAPTER 12

BONUS JOLT:
MOTIVATING OTHERS

WE DIDN'T LIGHT THE FIRE, IT WAS ALWAYS BURNING SINCE THE WORLD'S BEEN TURNING

"If your actions inspire others to dream more, learn more, do more and become more, you are a leader."
—JOHN QUINCY ADAMS

The purpose of this bonus chapter is to get you thinking about motivating others in business. When we talk about motivating others, we're talking about motivating people, like your family, your friends, and your employees. We're also talking about motivating your vendors, suppliers, and partners. All of these people will be essential for ensuring that you have a successful and prosperous business.

You may have noticed that a campfire does not light itself. You can set out the wood in a little arrangement of logs and carefully watch it all day and night, but it will not suddenly burst into flames.

It has to be lit. Much the same applies to you as a leader of your organization—you have to light the fire with all of the people you interact with. Like it or not, it is part of your responsibility.

Employees need to be motivated and need to have things to be motivated about. One CEO we met with said, "Well, if I have to motivate people, then I probably hired the wrong people." We cannot disagree with that more. Each and every one of us in our work have always needed and longed for a manager or leader who was positive, upbeat, and motivational. Some of us were lucky enough to have them, while others of us weren't.

YOUR FAMILY

We believe that the first step in creating a motivational environment is to start at home. Here are couple of questions that you really want to consider about your family, because, as the saying in the South often goes, "If momma is not happy, ain't nobody happy." How do you go about motivating and influencing your family so that they will support you and have your back while you go through the arduous journey of starting or running your own business as an entrepreneur? Here are a few things to think about.

Buy-in. One of the key aspects of motivation is to get buy-in from the other people you're involved with. You need to get buy-in from your family, which means, first of all, you need to get buy-in from your husband or your wife. We are speaking first and foremost in terms of getting the support you need. We have met many people who tell us they did not have a spouse at home who was supportive of the business or of them being an entrepreneur.

How do you get buy-in? The first step is open and honest communication. If you want to start a business, then you need to talk to your spouse about it in great depth in order to discuss how it is going to impact everyone involved. Find out how they feel about it and if they're willing to be supportive of you starting and/or running a business. The other question is, why are you running or starting a business—how is your family going to be financially supported? Is your partner or spouse willing to serve that role?

Another way to get buy-in is to ask your family's opinion, thoughts, and ideas about the business you are going to start. When people have a say and are able to give their opinion and feedback, they are often much more likely to buy into the ideas. The next element is to get support from your family, which could include your children, your brothers, sisters, and other relatives. Be open and honest about what you're trying to do. Talk about what you are doing, how it will affect them positively—short term, mid term, and long term—and share your vision with them. It's fascinating how often people are willing to go along when they know what the plan is and what the vision is meant to be.

It is also a good idea to think about how you being an entrepreneur may affect your family, both in positive ways and short-term negative ways. You may have to sacrifice your time in order to build a business, which may affect family members in different ways. Make sure they are aware of that and that you keep the lines of communication open.

Support. It is also important to talk with your family about how they can support your business and how you can support them as you go through the process of starting and running a business. Define what support means to you and your family. Does support mean financial support? Emotional support? Logistical support? Does it mean that you're asking your family to actually work in the business or on the business as you build it, or are you asking for them to commit their time and energy and effort as well? Or are you asking them to take a support role without being involved at all? These are questions you need to ask yourself in terms of family support. Define expectations before you start.

What's in it for them? When we do training for sales professionals, we often tell them that they have to think about how their product or service benefits the customer. We jokingly refer to it as radio station WIIFM, which stands for what is in it for me? What is in it for your family, both as a family unit and as individuals within your family? How will having and owning a business benefit your spouse in the short term, mid term, and long term? How will it benefit your children? Do you see your business as a kind of business that will be a legacy and one in which your children will actually be part of at some point in the future? Then talk to them about it, letting them know openly and honestly what would be in it for them.

One advantage of owning your own business is that you will have some scheduling freedom to make time to attend important family events, such as school activities, children's football games, and other significant moments in your children's life. Some people who have more traditional jobs do not have that kind of flexibility, so it definitely can be an added benefit. One of our friends owns a company where he is able to work from anywhere geographically. So every summer he and his family go stay in a beach house at the Jersey shore, and they are able to have a great time because he can do work from a remote location at the beach.

Don't ignore their needs. Unfortunately, the classic stereotype of most entrepreneurs is the one who misses almost all of their family's important events. They are not there for the school play, the soccer game, or the important birthday. You are building a business and it's a lot of hard work, time, and commitment, but just make sure that while you're doing that you don't ignore the needs of your husband, your wife, or your children. This can cause a great deal of stress and tension in the family. In the end you will not get the support you need in order to be successful. Make sure to work together on this.

Communicate. Although it seems obvious, it is important to communicate on a regular basis with everyone in your family about what it is that you're doing and how it's impacting them. Make sure to talk to your family members, both one on one and as a group, to make sure they are happy and that your business is not impacting them in negative ways.

You're not a mind reader and neither are they. The only way to really learn what's going on is to ask them. Have open and honest discussions about the challenges each person in the family faces and about what's going on in their lives. We honestly believe that entrepreneurs can have happier families because entrepreneurs have a lot more freedom of choice than people who are working nine to five. The channels of communication need to remain open in order to navigate the fast-paced life of being an entrepreneur.

MOTIVATE YOUR EMPLOYEES AND TEAM MEMBERS

Once you feel like you have your family situation well in hand, it is important to then consider how to get your employees and team members excited and motivated. We are frankly amazed at how many horror stories we hear from people working in companies about managers who are unappreciative, demotivating, and don't really seem to care about how employees perceive their work or the company. We are asking you to please not to be that person.

Some people have had the experience of working for horrible bosses, and some people have had the experience of working for bosses who changed their life in a positive way. Make sure you are the second kind of boss, the one who changes lives for the better. How do you go about motivating employees and creating a motivational environment? Here are some tips in order to achieve this.

Communicate the plan. One of the things we find tremendously motivating for employees is for them to actually not be kept in the dark. The biggest complaint we hear from employees at companies is that they don't know what is going on and no one bothers to tell them. Most employees view this as a form of disrespect, because they do, in fact, need to know what the company is doing and where the company is headed.

In earlier chapters we talked about the importance of having a mission and a vision, and knowing the purpose of your business. The next step is to communicate that to every single employee within your organization. You can communicate these plans through e-mail, training programs, new-hire orientation programs, town hall meetings, conference calls, and newsletters. Of course, each of these approaches is going to be customized depending on the number of employees you have. However, please do not overlook this important aspect of motivating employees, even if you have a small team of employees. Everyone would like to know and be in the loop.

What do they want? It's been said, "The best way to get what you want is to help other people get what they want." Here is the big question: what does each individual employee want? The answer is different for each person. Some people may want to move up and be promoted, while others would like to stay in the current job they have. Some people want more intellectual challenge, which for them is a chance to do really exciting work. Some people would like to do the same job every single day and are perfectly happy with doing so. Some people love their jobs, they are great at them, and they can really shine where they are.

The key to motivating employees is to find out what they want. We often say that if we laid ten padlocks out on a desk, they would all look exactly the same, but each padlock has a different key. It's much the same with people: you have to find out the key to their motivation. How do you go about doing that? First of all, you need to have ongoing communication with each direct report so you can find out what it is that they want. Hey, here is an idea: why don't you just ask them? Not surprisingly, most people will tell you exactly what it is that they want. Some people, of course, will just shrug because they don't really know what they want and they haven't really given it much thought.

If you want to have a team of highly motivated employees, then one of the secret keys is to find out what each one of them wants and start them down that road. Once each person is convinced that they're closer to getting what they want, then they will be extremely self-motivated, excited, and fired up. I'm sure you've heard the old saying, "You can lead a horse to water but you can't make him drink." That may be true, but in this case when we find out what they want, that convinces them to want to drink on their own. Meet with each employee privately one on one and ask them about their short-, mid-, and long-term goals for their career, and ask about their short-, mid-, and long-term goals for their personal life too, if they're willing to share them.

Individual development plans. We believe that a very powerful tool for helping and motivating employees is to develop with them through an individual development plan. The individual development plan is the product of a discussion we've previously had with them, where we asked them about their short-term, mid-term, and long-term goals, professionally speaking. We then have a conversation to determine what the best approach would be to help them develop the skill sets they are looking for in order to help them achieve their goals. We then need to follow up to see how their plans are going. Keep in mind that in order for an individual development plan to work, we have to follow up, otherwise the employee believes we are just creating smoke and mirrors. By following up we are making a serious commitment to that person's individual development.

Another advantage of individual development plans is that it is the end of the dead-end job. Employees get frustrated when they feel like they cannot possibly move out of their position they are currently in. The individual development plan implies that if people learn new skills and improve, they have the possibility of growth. We know of many organizations where the employees are capable of doing much more and they are actually working at less than their potential. What has happened is that the company has not given them a chance to work at their full potential yet—they haven't given them development in order to do so.

Believe in them. One of the biggest complaints we hear from employees is that their bosses do not believe in their skills, knowledge, and abilities. Let's say, for example, that you meet with an employee and have your individual development plan meeting, and the employee tells you they eventually would like to take over the company (after you retire, of course). In some cases you may believe that to be a real possibility, while in other cases you may not. But keep in mind that sometimes your judgment may not be correct. What you should do as a motivational tool is give that person the benefit of the doubt. Believe in them, because that is a motivating thought, when someone knows that you believe in them and their potential.

We often have people in our training seminars who say, "Oh, that's ridiculous—what if my cleaning person wants to become the CEO?" Well, what right do we have to stomp on that person's dreams? If someone wants to be the CEO, then let them make the effort. Both of us have heard of many companies where a person who started out as receptionist became a key executive or even the CEO. Don't stomp on someone's dreams—it's not your right and it's not fair. If they say they want to eventually run the company one day after you retire, then say, "Okay, if that is your goal, let's do an analysis of the skills you will need in order to effectively run the company." You then make a list of skills required to be in that role and have that employee start to work on developing those skills. Make it clear that there are no guarantees about what will happen in the future; you're not saying they will have the role, you're just saying you're going to help them prepare for the future.

Another possibility is that you may develop skill sets with an employee who will not stay with the company, but they will end up going somewhere else while using their newfound skills. That should be okay too. In fact, research shows that the newer generation of workers will not stay to collect a gold watch at retirement. They will hop from one company to another, gaining new skills in each company and using those new skills to get promoted to yet another. The good news is that research shows that while the new generation of employees may not stay forever, they will stay longer if they are receiving development and learning new skills.

How do we ensure that each of these folks gets the development they deserve? Once we've identified what it is they need to learn, we need to get them the training and development they desire. Yes, we know this is a bigtime resource commitment on your part—we get that. But it is well worth the investment, because when you own and run a company you can't do everything yourself. You are eventually going to have to rely on others to do things for you. You want to make sure that those other people who are doing things for you are motivated, committed, and loyal.

Rewards and incentives. One more element of motivating employees is to make sure that they are rewarded and get incentives for performing well. Rewards can take many forms, and one of the forms of rewards is money. Money would obviously include raises and bonuses, as well as other forms of financial reward, including stock options. However, there are many other kinds of rewards and incentives that may not be related directly to money. For example, an opportunity to participate or work on a certain project could be a form of reward if that's what the person really wants; a change in job function or opportunity can be a form of reward.

We also strongly believe in the power of the complement, and we're puzzled as to why so many leaders are reluctant to say thank you and express appreciation to employees for work well done. We often talk to employees who come in early and who are never late, and yet they are never told thank you or receive any appreciation for the hard work that they do. We often wonder if leaders have a budget for thank yous (thank yous are free). Don't be stingy with expressing your appreciation. When people feel appreciated, they feel motivated and want to work harder.

Shawn was working at one company and asked his boss how he was doing. His boss said, "You are doing well." Shawn said, "How would I know that?" His boss said, "I will tell you when you screw up." Shawn then said, "Well, but I need a compliment every now and then." His boss replied, "I am not going to compliment you for something we pay you to do." Ridiculous. Please take the time to thank someone verbally for their hard work, leave a message on their voicemail or write a handwritten thank-you note specifically expressing your appreciation.

You may want to also think about investing in items that are small thank yous, such as $10.00 or $20.00 gift cards to Starbucks or Target, for example. How does this work? When someone does a great job, walk over to them, thank them for their hard work, and hand them a gift card. Although these are low in terms of dollar expense, they have a high perceived value when given as a reward.

THE ENVIRONMENT YOU CREATE

All of us have been visitors to organizations where we walk into the building or department and we can almost immediately tell that it's an energetic, positive, upbeat environment where people are enjoying their work and having fun. We have also had the opposite experience, where we walked into an environment that just seemed low energy, negative, and filled with tension. How does this happen?

The leader sets the tone, or maybe better said, the leader sets the corporate culture of the company. The corporate culture and environment in the office is either set deliberately or accidentally, but it is always set by the leader. It is our desire that you create an environment that is deliberately upbeat, optimistic, and dynamic. How do you go about doing that?

Provide training. We have noticed that companies that regularly sponsor training classes at work end up with employees who are upbeat, optimistic, and positive because they're constantly learning new things. In addition to training being motivating and stimulating, it also provides an opportunity for the team to get together as a group, creating a bonding experience.

Trips. When people go as a group to industry conferences, to trade shows, or to any other business-related trips, they have fun getting to know each other better, as well as bonding as a group.

Activities. Most employees know they have to work hard in order to be successful. That being said, it is a good idea to occasionally schedule activities in your workplace. These activities could be a team lunch, a team meeting, a themed office day, such as jeans day or casual day or your favorite sports team jersey day, or a potluck lunch where everybody brings their favorite dish. Just try to think of fun activities that can be done in the office as a group that would help add to the fun of working.

You may also want to think about occasionally having outdoor activities for the entire team, such as everyone going to play miniature golf, bowling, or going on a picnic. Keep in mind, however, that these activities should be done during work hours, not on a weekend. We also suggest sponsoring company events at least twice a year, where you can invite the employees and their spouses, partners, and families to a local amusement park, minor league baseball game, or to a company picnic. Please don't miss the important aspect of planning these activities. The activities are not activities just for the sake of activities; they are activities to create a better bond amongst the team and to create a positive family environment in the office.

- *Celebrations.* It is important to celebrate many things, because celebrations are motivating. There are several things you may want to think about celebrating.

- *Employee anniversaries.* It is a good idea to celebrate the anniversary of employees. One of our clients in Alabama has a monthly meeting where everyone stops work so they can have cake and ice cream, celebrating the people who have had a work anniversary that month. Employees love this monthly meeting and feel appreciated and acknowledged.

- *Employee birthdays.* Take the time to get together as a group, have everyone sign a card, and celebrate each employee's birthday. The small celebrations make a difference.

- *Employee awards.* You may want to have annual employee awards, like the employee of the year, salesperson of the year, customer-service person of the year, and team of the year. Or you could do

these on a monthly basis as well. We have watched
many employee award banquets and have seen the
excitement, passion, and tears when people gave their
acceptance speeches. Recognizing people for their
work is motivating and uplifting.

Serve them. As a leader, it is important to help people who work
for you. Do them small favors. Bring in doughnuts one morning when
everyone has been working hard. Give someone a ride home every now
and then if they need one. If they are facing adversity and need help,
then provide the help they need. If they need time off to take care of
something in their family, grant them the time off they need. Do whatever you can to serve them and make them feel like they are valuable.

Have fun. If you have fun, then they will have fun. Let them
know they can work hard and have fun at the same time. It doesn't
have to be an either-or choice, it can definitely be a both-and.

> *"A sure sign of a soul-based workplace is excitement,*
> *enthusiasm, real passion; not manufactured passion,*
> *but real involvement. And there's very little fear."*
> —DAVID WHYTE

WORK IT!

What do you need to do to get more buy-in from your family?

_____

_____

_____

_____

_____

_____

_____

Which employees do you need to create an individual action plan for?

_____

_____

_____

_____

_____

_____

_____

What kinds of rewards can you provide?

_____

_____

_____

_____

_____

_____

What activities can you do to create an office environment that is more fun?

_____

_____

_____

_____

_____

_____

EPILOGUE

We want you to imagine a year from now—just a mere 365 days from this point in time. That is not so long from now.

In a year from now, your business can be greater than anything you have ever imagined.

You can be a millionaire, with your business growing and revenue tripling every month.

You can have financial freedom for you and your family.

You can be on the cover of *Inc.* magazine.

You can take dream vacations and live in the house that was on your vision board.

You can be giving back to charities and to your community.

You can help friends and family.

You can do anything you want.

You can be happy, healthy, and joyful.

The choice is now yours. Know and understand that you are the architect of your own life. Today is the day to ignite your entrepreneurial spirit.

CONTACT US

Please contact us for:

- Speaking at your next meeting

- Full-day and half-day training programs

- Executive coaching

- Life coaching

- Consulting

- Online learning programs

- Licensing our programs

New Light Learning and Development Inc.
www.sldoyle.com
sldoyle1@aol.com
610.857.4742

Thanks, and have a fantastic day.

A RESOURCE READING LIST FOR YOU

Leadership

- *Leadership Secrets of Colin Powell* by Orin Harrari
- *#Girlboss* by Sophia Amoruso
- *A Passion for Excellence: The Leadership Difference* by Nancy Austin and Thomas J. Peters
- *Executive Charisma: Six Steps to Mastering the Art of Leadership* by D. A. Benton
- *The 5 Dysfunctions of a Team* by Patrick Lencioni
- *Lions Don't Need to Roar* by D. A. Benton
- *Monday Morning Leadership: 8 Mentoring Sessions You Can't Afford to Miss* by David Cottrell
- *Principle Centered Leadership* by Stephen R. Covey
- *Leadership Is an Art* by Max Depree
- *The 21 Indispensable Qualities of a Leader: Becoming the Person Others Will Want to Follow* by John Maxwell
- *Good to Great: Why Some Companies Make the Leap...and Others Don't* by Jim Collins
- *On Becoming a Leader* by Warren Bennis

- *True North: Discover Your Authentic Leadership* by Bill George and Peter Sims

- *Creating Magic: 10 Common Sense Leadership Strategies from a Life at Disney* by Lee Cockerell

- *The Mary Kay Way: Timeless Principles from America's Greatest Woman Entrepreneur* by Mary Kay Ash

- *Jumpstart Your Leadership* by Shawn Doyle

- *Winning* by Jack Welch and Suzy Welch

- *It's Your Ship: Management Techniques from the Best Damn Ship in the Navy* by Michael Abrashoff

- *Managing the Generation Mix, 2nd Edition (Manager's Pocket Guide Series)* by Carolyn A. Martin and Bruce Tulgan

- *Twist of Faith: The Story of Anne Beiler, Founder of Auntie Anne's Pretzels* by Anne Beiler

- *Losing My Virginity: How I Survived, Had Fun, and Made a Fortune Doing Business My Way* by Richard Branson

- *Steve Jobs: The Exclusive Biography* by Walter Isaacson

- *Nuts! Southwest Airlines' Crazy Recipe for Business and Personal Success* by Kevin Freiberg and Jackie Freiberg

- *Shackleton's Way: Leadership Lessons from the Great Antarctic Explorer* by Margot Morrell, Stephanie Capparell, and Alexandra Shackleton

COMMUNICATION SKILLS

- *The Platinum Rule: Discover the Four Basic Business Personalities and How They Can Lead You to Success* by Tony Alessandra

- *Working with Emotional Intelligence* by Daniel Goleman

- *PeopleSmart: Developing Your Interpersonal Intelligence* by Melvin L. Silberman

- *Crucial Conversations: Tools for Talking When Stakes Are High* by Kerry Patterson, Joseph Grenny, Ron McMillan, and Al Switzler

- *Fierce Conversations: Achieving Success at Work and in Life One Conversation at a Time* by Susan Scott

- *Death by Meeting: A Leadership Fable...About Solving the Most Painful Problem in Business* by Patrick Lencioni

- *The Coward's Guide to Conflict: Empowering Solutions for Those Who Would Rather Run Than Fight* by Timothy E. Ursiny

- *The Quick and Easy Way to Effective Speaking* by Dale Carnegie

- *Speak to Win: How to Present with Power in Any Situation* by Brian Tracy

- *Games People Play: The Basic Handbook of Transactional Analysis* by Eric Berne

- *The Power of Body Language: How to Succeed in Every Business and Social Encounter* by Tonya Reiman

- *Charisma: Seven Keys to Developing the Magnetism that Leads to Success* by Tony Alessandra

- *Trailblazers: How Top Business Leaders Are Accelerating Results through Inclusion and Diversity* by Redia Anderson and Lenora Billings-Harris

CREATIVITY AND INNOVATION

- *Cracking Creativity: The Secrets of Creative Genius* by Michael Michalko

- *Jamming: The Art and Discipline of Business Creativity* by John Kao

- *Coloring Outside the Lines: Business Thoughts on Creativity, Sales, and Marketing* by Jeff Tobe

- *Ignore Everybody: and 39 Other Keys to Creativity* by Hugh MacLeod

- *Creativity: Flow and the Psychology of Discovery and Invention* by Mihaly Csikszentmihalyi

- *The Artist's Way* by Julia Cameron

- *Six Thinking Hats* by Edward de Bono

- *How to Think Like Leonardo da Vinci: Seven Steps to Genius Every Day* by Michael Gelb

- *Eiffel's Tower: The Thrilling Story Behind Paris's Beloved Monument and the Extraordinary World's Fair That Introduced It* by Jill Jonnes

- *A Whack on the Side of the Head: How You Can Be More Creative* by Roger von Oech

- *Jumpstart Your Creativity* by Shawn Doyle and Steven Rowell

MOTIVATION

- *Jumpstart Your Motivation: Ten Jolts to Get Motivated and Stay Motivated* by Shawn Doyle

- *Are You Living or Existing?* by Kimanzi Constable

- *Quiet Strength: The Principles, Practices, and Priorities of a Winning Life* by Tony Dungy and Nathan Whitaker

- *Finding Your Voice* by Joel Boggess

- *The Monk Who Sold His Ferrari: A Fable About Fulfilling Your Dreams & Reaching Your Destiny* by Robin Sharma

- *Just Blow It Up: Firepower for Living an Unlimited Life* by Dixie Gillaspie

- *Finding Your Own North Star: Claiming the Life You Were Meant to Live* by Martha Beck

- *Live Your Dreams* by Les Brown

- *Back from Heaven's Front Porch* by Danny Bader

- *The Power of Positive Thinking* by Norman Vincent Peale

- *A Better Way to Live: Og Mandino's Own Personal Story of Success, Featuring 17 Rules to Live By* by Og Mandino

- *You Are a Badass* by Jen Sincero

- *Excuses Begone!: How to Change Lifelong, Self-Defeating Thinking Habits* by Wayne W. Dyer

- *Unlimited Power: The New Science of Personal Achievement* by Anthony Robbins

- *Man's Search for Meaning* by Viktor E. Frankl

- *The Secret* by Rhonda Byrne

- *The Biology of Belief* by Bruce H. Lipton

- *Think and Grow Rich* by Napoleon Hill

- *The Game of Life & How to Play It* by Florence Scovel Shinn

- *The Seven Spiritual Laws of Success: A Practical Guide to the Fulfillment of Your Dreams* by Deepak Chopra

- *How to Win Friends and Influence People* by Dale Carnegie

- *Personhood* by Leo Buscaglia

- *Possibility Thinking* by Robert Schuller

- *The Richest Man in Babylon* by George Clason

- *You'll See It When You Believe It* by Wayne W. Dyer

- *Super Power Memory* by Harry Lorayne

- *Do What You Love, The Money Will Follow* by Marsha Sinetar

TIME MANAGEMENT

- *The 7 Habits of Highly Effective People* by Stephen R. Covey

- *How to Get Control of Your Time and Life* by Alan Lakein

- *Get Your Act Together* by Peggy Jones

- *Doing It Now* by Edwin Bliss

ABOUT THE AUTHORS

Shawn Doyle, CSP, is a learning and development professional who has a passion for human potential. He has an avid belief in the concept of lifelong learning. For the last twenty-two years, Shawn has spent his time developing and implementing training programs on team building, communication, creativity, and leadership. Shawn's training programs help people become more effective in the workplace and in their lives. His clients have included numerous Fortune 500 companies, and his awards and honors are extensive. Shawn is the author of sixteen inspirational books.

Rachael Doyle was born into a family that has had multiple generations of successful entrepreneurs. In her early teens she worked in the family business in several different roles. In her late twenties, she cofounded and ran a successful photography business in Michigan for several years with a partner. Rachael has worked in her own business or for other businesses for over three decades and has learned many valuable lessons from her experience. She has a passion for lifelong learning and has an impressive collection of business and motivational books, all of which she has read, many of them more than once.